S0-AYV-607

GAMBLING TIMES PRESENTS

WINNING SYSTEMS AND METHODS

Volume Two

A GAMBLING TIMES BOOK

DISTRIBUTED BY
LYLE STUART
Secaucus, N.J.

GAMBLING TIMES PRESENTS WINNING SYSTEMS AND METHODS— VOLUME TWO

Copyright © 1984 by Gambling Times Incorporated

All rights reserved. No part of this book may be reproduced or utilized by any means, electronic or mechanical, including photocopying, recording or by any information storage or retrieval system, without permission from Gambling Times Incorporated, except by a newspaper or magazine reviewer who wants to quote brief passages in connection with a review. All inquiries should be addressed to Gambling Times Incorporated, 1018 N. Cole Ave., Hollywood, CA 90038.

Distributed by
Lyle Stuart, Inc.

ISBN: 0-89746-037-5

Manufactured in the United States of America
Printed and Bound by Kingsport Press
First Printing—January 1984

Editor: *Kelley D. Ritchey*
Cover Design: *Terry Robinson*
Cover Illustration: *Laurie Newell*

All material presented in this book is offered as information to the reader. No inducement to gamble is intended or implied.

ATTENTION: GAMING ENTREPRENEURS AND OTHER BUSINESSES

Gambling Times' books are available at quantity discounts with bulk purchase for educational, business, or sales promotions use. Very large orders can have special covers with your business imprint. What better gift than a good book which is enjoyed and treasured by the recipient? For information, write to Director of Book Publishing, Gambling Times Incorporated, 1018 N. Cole Ave., Hollywood, CA 90038.

Other *Gambling Times* Books
Available—Current Releases
(See page 125 for details.)

Poker Books

According to Doyle
by Doyle Brunson
Caro On Gambling by Mike Caro
Caro's Book of Tells by Mike Caro
The GT Official Rules of Poker
by Mike Caro
Poker For Women by Mike Caro
Poker Without Cards by Mike Caro
Wins, Places and Pros
by Tex Sheahan

Blackjack Books

The Beginner's Guide to Winning
Blackjack by Stanley Roberts
The GT Guide to Blackjack
by Stanley Roberts and others
Million Dollar Blackjack
by Ken Uston

Casino Games

The GT Guide to Casino Games
by Len Miller
The GT Guide to Craps
by N.B. Winkless, Jr.

General Interest Books

According to GT: The Rules of
Gambling Games
by Stanley Roberts

The GT Guide to Gaming Around
the World
The GT Guide to Systems That
Win, Volumes I and II
The GT Guide to Winning
Systems, Volumes I
GT Presents Winning Systems and
Methods, Volumes I and II
The Mathematics of Gambling
by Dr. Edward O. Thorp
Odds: Quick and Simple
by Mike Caro
P$yching Out Vegas
by Marvin Karlins, Ph.D.
Winning By Computer
by Dr. Donald Sullivan

Sports Betting Books

The GT Guide to Basketball
Handicapping by Barbara Nathan
The GT Guide to Football
Handicapping by Bob McCune
The GT Guide to Greyhound
Racing by William E. McBride
The GT Guide to Harness Racing
by Igor Kusyshyn, Ph.D.,
Al Stanley and Sam Dragich
The GT Guide to Jai Alai
by William R. Keevers
The GT Guide to Thoroughbred
Racing by R.G. Denis

The following *Gambling Times* books
are scheduled for release in September 1984:

Poker Books

Caro's Poker Encyclopedia
by Mike Caro

**Free Money: How to Win in the
Cardrooms of California**
by Michael Wiesenberg

The Railbird by Rex Jones

Tales Out of Tulsa
by Bobby Baldwin

**World Class Poker, Play by
Play** by Mike Caro

General Interest Books

Caro On Computer Gambling
by Mike Caro

The GT Quiz Book
by Mike Caro

How the Superstars Gamble
by Ron Delpit

**How to Win at Gaming
Tournaments** by Haven Earle Haley

**You're Comped: How to Be a
Casino Guest** by Len Miller

Sports Betting Books

**Fast Track to
Harness Racing Profits**
by Mark Cramer

**Fast Track to
Thoroughbred Profits**
by Mark Cramer

TABLE OF CONTENTS

Section One
CASINO GAMES

This section contains an analysis of keno, a strategy for beating the progressive video poker machines, and a look at blackjack in the Caribbean.

Section One
CASINO GAMES

Chapter 1

More Odds Against You

by Michael Wiesenberg

Keno is a great casino game for the *low* roller. For $1, you can win $50,000. It takes little effort to play. You don't have to watch what those funny little spotted cubes are doing and figure out which proposition to take, you don't have to count blackjack cards, you don't have to keep pushing bets onto the roulette layout. You don't even have to get your exercise by continually pulling a slot machine handle.

But you *do* have to give something up when you play keno.

In exchange for a chance to win lots of money, you have to give an edge to the house. The problem is, most players don't know how much they're giving up. My article, "Keno: The Odds Against You," printed in the July 1979 issue of *Gambling Times,* presented the house edge and breakdown of the popular tickets being offered at that time by the casinos. Since then, the casinos have changed the payoffs. The house edge ranges from well over 50% for the house to a ticket that actually offers the player a positive expectation. (The two extremes, by the way, are not found in Nevada, where the edge ranges from under 20% to over 40%.)

In general, however, the house edge keeps getting worse. In the mid-60s, the take in the Nevada casinos was in the 15% to 20% range. Then the clubs introduced the higher-paying "specials," increasing the cost of a ticket from 50ᶜ to 55ᶜ, and the edge moved into the range of 20% to 25%. They raised the price of an average ticket again in the late 60s, and the edge crept upward.

Until the 1970s, keno ticket payoffs were mostly standardized throughout Nevada. Six on a 70ᶜ eight-spot ticket paid the same at Caesars Palace in Las Vegas as at Harrah's Tahoe. When the maximum payout was increased from $25,000 to $50,000 the edge moved up again, and at most clubs in Nevada it has settled around 30%. Clubs frequently introduce new tickets, each with its own set of payoffs, each often different from any other club's ticket, and, surprisingly, many with different house edges.

Do the clubs not know how to figure and adjust their edge? If so, a club may accidentally introduce a ticket that favors the player.

A License to Steal?

How *do* the casinos get away with their large take? They claim high overheads in the game, but in actuality the ignorance of the players lets them keep it up. If enough players learned how much of an edge they were giving the house, they'd quit playing keno and try something with a better return on their gambling dollar.

For example, you can now win much more on a slot machine than on any keno ticket. There seems to be no upper limit on slot payoffs. A cool million has been won by one pull of the handle on a progressive machine. For $1 on an eight-spot keno ticket you can win $18,000 to $25,000, and yet the chances of lining up all the jackpot symbols on a four-reel slot machine (paying ten times as much and more) are approximately the same as catching eight out of eight on the keno ticket. The edge on most of those progressive machines is under 10%, and they pay off much more frequently than do keno tickets.

Now, it *is* true that players in other games bet more *per unit of time* than in keno (a slot machine handle is pulled every few seconds, while a keno game typically lasts up to fifteen minutes; blackjack hands and dice decisions come every few minutes or less), and thus to earn what they consider a reasonable *hourly* rate, the casinos impose a high edge, and maybe they do need that to keep the game running. If the casinos offered reasonable prizes, they'd find more people willing to play. Why play a game in which you can win "only" $50,000—and that with prohibitive odds—when you can win 20 times that on a slot machine?

If casinos offered prizes ten times as high on keno as now, and that attracted ten times as many players, they could cut the edge to less than 10% and actually make *more* money.

Some of the tickets in the accompanying tables are marked "Proposed." These are tickets I have devised that the casinos could offer, which would pay in the same ball park as the slots, and would not have such a high edge. And if they used electronic keno equipment, they could run games much faster, and reduce operating costs. They could run the games the way they do now, except draw the numbers and make the punchouts with a machine similar to a video slot machine. (The electronic keno games—really forms of slot machines—that currently exist, each played by one player, typically offer a maximum payout of $10,000. Make them progressive. They'll get as much play as the progressive jackpot video slot machines.)

How the Casinos Make Money on Keno

Casinos make money at keno by not returning enough when you win. For example, when you win with a one-spot ticket, you get back $3 for your $1 bet. You had 20 chances out of 80 to pick the right number, or one out of four. That's the same as three to one against you. You *profit* on a win by $2 ($3 payoff minus the $1 you paid for the ticket), so you get 2:1 on a 3:1 proposition. What you should get (if the game had no house edge) is $4.

If you play lots of these one-spot tickets, you should win one time in four. That is, three times you lose $1, and one time you win $2. In four plays, your *net loss* is $1. For each play, you lose one-fourth of that, or 25¢. Divide that by the cost of the ticket to find the house edge: $.25/1.00 = .25 = 25\%$.

The figuring becomes more complicated when you deal with tickets with more spots, but the principle is the same. You figure the chances of each catch, and multiply that by what it pays. For example, on a two-spot ticket, the chance of catching one number is 20/80. After you get one, you have 19 chances out of 79. The chances of getting both are those two numbers multiplied, or 20/80 times 19/79, which equals about .0601. For a $1 bet, most casinos pay $12. Multiply $12 by .0601 and you get .7212. That is, for every $1 you bet on a two-spot, you get back just over 72ᶜ. The casino keeps the rest. This represents its edge, .2788, or 27.88%.

Deciding Which Ticket to Play

To decide which ticket to play, you need to know more than just the house edge. You are not bucking the high house edge of keno to win a few dollars. You want to win a large prize, say at least 1000 times the price of the ticket.

For example, the Circus Circus 15-spot keno ticket returns only 4ᶜ out of every dollar wagered in the form of 1000 times (or more) the price of the ticket. That is, of the approximately 73ᶜ you get back for every $1 bet, you get 69ᶜ by catching either six, seven, eight, nine, or ten spots. Catching 11, 12, 13, 14, or 15 is worth only 4ᶜ of the return. And the odds against winning at least 1000 times the cost of the ticket are 76844:1!

Now look at the Sands' special eight-spot. Notice that the house edge on this ticket is higher than the 15, yet it returns 43ᶜ out of every dollar wagered in the form of 1000 times (or more) the price of the ticket. And it's "only" about 6067:1 against winning at least 1000 times the cost of the ticket. The eight-spot doesn't have as many small pays, but it's a lot easier to win the big money. What this means is that the eight-spot ticket is "top-weighted," while the 15 is "bottom-weighted."

As an example of how high the house edge can get, Caesars Tahoe has a 20-spot ticket they call "The Roaring Twenties." For $5, catches 20, 19, 18, 17, and 16 all win $50,000; 15 wins $25,000; 14, 13, and 12 win $12,500, $5000, and $1000, respectively; 11, 10, nine, eight, and seven win, $200, $50, $25, $10, and $5; six and five paying nothing; three and two each pay $5; catching exactly one spot wins $10, and catching none wins $50. Looks great at first glance.

Catch 16 or more and win $50,000, but that's a 1,471,858,715:1 shot! And you even win $50 for catching no spots. That happens once every 823 tickets you play. The edge on this ticket is 40.03%. It's only 1.69:1 against winning something on the ticket, but you'll win $5000 or more only once in 110,595 tickets, representing a return of 1ᶜ for every $1 you wager.

Which would you rather do? Win a few bucks, or win big? Look at the breakdowns (in Table 1-1) done by the computer for many popular tickets and make your decision. My recommendation is to play the tickets that offer the greatest chance of winning at least 1000 times the cost of the ticket; that is, those that offer the largest return on your investment in the form of winning at least 1000 times the cost of the ticket.

Some Typical Tickets

Table 1-1 shows some typical tickets. Those from Nevada have a house edge ranging from under 18% to over 40%. The Montana tickets listed are all over 40%. (Some keep over 99%; yet one variation actually offers the *player* the edge. More on that later.)

To list the maximum number of tickets, the figures are presented in compact (and somewhat cryptic) form. Here's how to read the Table. The first column ("Ticket") is the name of the club, and sometimes the club's special name for the ticket. The second column is the cost of the ticket.

The third column lists the payouts for *all* catches, from all the numbers to none. For example, under "6-Spot Tickets," the *payouts* for Caesars Tahoe "All Pay" ticket (all catches win) are listed as 1200,60,3,1,.50,.50,1.50. Notice that there are seven entries. This means that six out of six pays $1200, five out of six pays $60, four pays $3, three pays $1, two and one pay 50ᶜ each,

9

Table 1-1

Some Typical Keno Tickets

	Cost	Payouts	Edge	1000x	RET	100x	RET
3-Spot Tickets							
Holiday Casino (LV)							
catch all	1.25	64,-,-,-	28.96	—	—	—	—
4-Spot Tickets							
Holiday Casino (LV)							
catch all	1.25	290,-,-,-	28.93	—	—	325	.71
Showboat (LV) Spec.	.75	125,3.5,-,-,-	28.76	—	—	325	.51
Sundance (LV)	1.00	112,4,1,-,-,-	27.13	—	—	44	.34
5-Spot Tickets							
Claim Jumper Saloon (Helena, MT)	.50	100,8,1,-,-,-	50.97	—	—	1550	13
Imperial Palace "All or Nothing"	1.75	1000,-,-,-,1.75	40.43	—	—	—	-;-
Caesars (LV) Gambler Special	10.00	11000,-,-,-,-,-	29.06	155	.71	1550	71
Holiday Casino (LV) catch all	1.25	1390,-,-,-,-	28.28	—	—	1550	.32
Showboat (LV) Spec.	1.00	720,14,1,-,-,-	28.24	—	—	1550	.46
Union Plaza (LV) High 5 Special	1.95	1499,-,-,-,1.95	27.71	—	—	1550	.50
Caesars (LV) all catches win	2.50	1250,25,2.50,.25,.25,2.50	17.78	—	—	1550	.32

(continued)

10

Table 1-1

6-Spot Tickets

Claim Jumper Saloon (Helena, MT)	.50	100,40,2.50,.50,-,-,-	45.40	—	—	7752 .03
Imperial Palace "All or Nothing"	1.75	4444,-,-,-,-,3.50	33.92	7752	.33	7752 .33
Caesars (LV) Gambler Special	10.00	30000,1000,-,-,-,-	30.35	7752	.39	309 .70
Holiday Casino (LV) catch all	1.25	6800,-,-,-,-,-	29.83	7752	.70	7752 .70
Harveys (Tahoe)	1.00	2500,100,3,-,-,-	28.24	7752	.32	309 .63
Caesars Tahoe Special	1.00	2600,100,3,-,-,-	26.95	7752	.34	309 .64
Caesars Tahoe Regular	1.00	1480,100,3,1,-,-	24.11	7752	.19	309 .50
Caesars Tahoe "All pay"	1.50	1200,60,3,1,.50,.50,1.50	23.88	—	—	7752 .10

7-Spot Tickets

Claim Jumper Saloon (Helena, MT)	.50	100,60,10,1,-,-,-	63.01	—	—	1320 .09
Imperial Palace "7 Come 11"	1.75	11000,-,-,-,-,7	36.03	40978	.15	40978 .15
Holiday Casino (LV) catch all	1.25	35000,-,-,-,-,-	31.67	40978	.68	40978 .68
Showboat (LV) Spec.	1.00	8000,380,20,1,-,-,-	30.16	40978	.20	1321 .47
Holiday Casino (LV) all win	2.00	5000,240,24,4,.80,.50,.50,2	29.11	40978	.06	1321 .15

(continued)

Table 1-1
Some Typical Keno Tickets

8-Spot Tickets	Cost	Payout	Edge	1000x	RET	100x	RET
Claim Jumper Saloon	.50	100,100,42,4.50,-,-,-,-	60.35	—	—	6067	.03
Imperial Palace (LV)	1.00	17000,1480,85,8,-,-,-,-	34.11	6067	.31	6067	.31
Showboat	1.00	20000,1480,80,9,-,-,-,-	32.16	6067	.32	6067	.32
Frontier (LV)	1.00	18000,1480,90,9,-,-,-,-	30.66	6067	.32	6067	.32
Riviera (LV)	1.00	18000,1500,90,9,-,-,-,-	30.34	6067	.32	6067	.32
Sahara (LV)	1.00	18000,1480,92,9,-,-,-,-	30.18	6067	.32	6067	.32
Sands (LV) Special	1.00	25000,2000,75,5,-,-,-,-	30.14	6067	.43	6067	.43
Hotel Fremont (LV)	1.00	25000,1480,80,9,-,-,-,-	29.98	6067	.35	6067	.35
Vegas World	1.40	25000,2300,120,12,-,-,-,-	29.91	6067	.34	6067	.34
Sands (LV)	1.00	19000,1500,90,9,-,-,-,-	29.90	6067	.32	6067	.32
Circus Circus (LV)	.75	15000,1117.50,67.50,6.75,-,-,-,-	29.63	6067	.33	6067	.33
Castaways (LV)	1.00	18000,1659,85,9,-,-,-,-	29.13	6067	.34	6067	.34
Harvey's (Tahoe)	1.00	18000,1650,90,9,-,-,-,-	27.93	6067	.34	6067	.34
Caesars Tahoe "King Ticket"*	93.00	50000,50000,9053,1429,98,20,-,-,-	26.77	—	—	6067	.09
Caesars (LV) Super Special	7.00	50000,13000,600,60,7,-,-,-,-	22.97	6067	.33	6067	.33
Proposed Special	1.00	100000,1000,100,5,-,-,-,-	7.68	6067	.60	394	.83

* Eight groups of one: 56 fives, 28 sixes, 8 sevens, 1 eight; all at regular $1 rate.

9-Spot Tickets	Cost	Payout	Edge	1000x	RET	100x	RET
Claim Jumper Saloon	.50	100,100,75,25,2,-,-,-,-	48.82	—	—	1599	.10
Sundance Hotel Spec.	1.00	40000,5000,400,36,2,-,-,-,-	30.03	30014	.19	1599	.43
Sundance Hotel Reg.	1.00	25000,4000,300,44,4,-,-,-,-	29.20	30014	.15	1599	.33
Showboat (LV)	1.00	20000,4000,280,44,3,.50,-,-,-	28.30	30014	.14	1599	.31
Caesars Tahoe "All pay"	1.50	20000,1950,300,20,3,1.50,.50,.50,1.50	24.93	30014	.05	1599	.17

(continued)

Table 1-1

10-Spot Tickets

		Payouts					
Claim Jumper Saloon	.50	100,100,100,70,10,1,-,-,-,-	41.37	—		570	.25
Desert Inn (LV)	1.50	37500,5700,1440,195,27,3,-,-,-,-	32.50	160439	.03	570	.37
Proposed Quarter# Million $ Special	1.00	250000,15000,1000,100,10,5,1,-,-,-,-	6.44	7059	.26	570	.42

12-Spot Tickets

Caesars Tahoe	1.00	25000,13000,2400,850,200,28,6,-,-,-,-,-	30.97	178655	.02	891	.30
Flamingo Hilton (LV)	2.00	50000,16000,2960,1200,64,10,-,-,-,-,-,-	30.27	178655	.01	891	.31
Harvey's (Tahoe) Special	1.50	29000,14500,3000,950,320,40,10, -,-,-,-,-,1.50	28.42	178655	.01	891	.29
Proposed Special	1.00	100000,7500,250,50,5,-,-,-,-	8.62	30014	.32	1599	.46

13-Spot Tickets

Sahara Las Vegas	1.00	36000,20000,8000,4000,720,80,16,1,-,-, -,-,-,-	30.54	47550	.09	3559	.28

15-Spot Tickets

Imperial Palace "Ginza Grabber"	2.25	50000,40000,30000,8225,3333,507,25,205, 27,25,2,25,-,-,-,-,2,25,4,50,27,25	36.11	76844	.02	6057	.06
Typical 15-spot	.75	30000,24000,18000,6000,1500,225,99,21,6, -,-,-,-,-,-,-	31.23	76844	.04	697	.24
Circus Circus (LV)	1.00	50000,50000,35000,8000,2400,240,75,21,8,2, -,-,-,-,-	26.71	76844	.04	6057	.07
Proposed Million Dollar Special	1.00	1000000,1000000,500000,250000, 17500,1000,100,10,5,-,-,-,-,-,-,-	10.94	6057	.54	697	.67

13

and catching *no* spots is worth $1.50. Dashes represent no pay. Thus, the Imperial Palace "7 Come 11" seven-spot ticket *payouts* are 11000,-,-,-,-,-,7. For $1.75, catching seven out of seven pays $11,000, all catches six down to one don't pay, and catching none is worth $7.

The fourth column is the house edge. For example, the Caesars Palace five-spot ticket on which all catches win has an edge of 17.78%.

The fifth column ("1000X") is the odds against winning 1000 times the cost of the ticket or more. The sixth is the return ("Ret") this represents, presenting how much of a $1 investment is returned in the form of a winner of 1000 times the cost of the ticket or more. For example, the Flamingo Hilton 12-spot costs $2. Catching all 12 is worth $50,000; 11 is worth $16,000; 10, $2960; and nine, $1200. To win at *least* 1000 times the cost of the ticket, you have to catch ten or more spots. The odds against this happening are 178655:1. Catching ten or more is worth a 1ᶜ return for every dollar invested.

The seventh column, "100x," and eight, "Ret," are similar. In the same example, 100 times the cost of the ticket is $200. The closest payout above $200 is $1200. The odds against catching at least nine spots on this ticket are 891:1. Catching nine, ten, 11, or 12 spots is worth 31ᶜ out of every $1 you care to invest on this ticket. That is, if you played millions and millions of these $2 twelve-spot tickets, and kept track of how many times you hit nine or more spots, you'd find that represented a return of 31ᶜ on every dollar you bet.

The two "Ret" columns are the most important in deciding which ticket to play. If the ticket you're interested in isn't listed, look for one with the same payouts.

Two Sleepers

Sometimes you find a "sleeper." In late December of 1980, the Tropicana advertised in the local papers a "Keno Holiday Special." You could play six spots for 75ᶜ, and win $2500 for catching six, $50 for five, $5 for four, and 50ᶜ for three. The house edge on this ticket was 8.69%! Unfortunately for smart keno players, this special was offered for only a month.

Keno is also played in some of the taverns of Montana. (Some clubs have poker, also.) The maximum payout per game is only $100 (and you can't wager more than 50ᶜ on any ticket), so you needn't start packing. In addition to tickets similar to Nevada's (except with a much higher edge), they have "split-choice" tickets, in which you try to predict exactly how many spots will be chosen in the top half of the layout.

Table 1-2 is a breakdown on all of the split-choice tickets. For example, a split-choice ticket specifying a catch of zero on top should return $12,823,377.46 for 50ᶜ, but it actually returns $100, giving the house an edge in excess of 99.999%.

Most split-choice tickets have a high house edge; except for a catch of exactly six or 14 spots on the top, the house always pays less than it should. The six and 14, however, each return about 15.6ᶜ *more* than they should. But, you only hit one of these once in about 40 tries. That means your positive expectation per ticket is about .38ᶜ. Since the rules specify $100 maximum payoff, if you play *several* tickets and hit them all you still get only $100. You would lose your edge by playing more than one ticket.

It may not be worth your time to sit around playing split-choice tickets for a third of a cent a game! That is, however, a better deal than any other keno ticket anywhere. If the word got around, everyone would play only those tickets (boy, would that be boring!), and the house would lose very, very slightly overall (a third of a cent every time someone hit one of them). Eventually they'd catch on, and change the payoffs on those two split-choice tickets.

Table 1-2

Montana's "Split-Choice" Keno Tickets

Catch	Pays	Should Pay	House Edge (%)
0	$100.00	$12823377.46	99.99 +
1	100.00	336613.66	99.97
2	100.00	19987.86	99.49
3	100.00	2016.32	95.04
4	75.00	307.74	75.62
5	40.00	66.78	40.10
6	20.00	19.84	—.78
7	5.00	7.88	36.54
8	3.00	4.11	27.08
9	1.50	2.80	46.35
10	1.00	2.46	59.35
11	1.50	2.80	46.35
12	3.00	4.11	27.08
13	5.00	7.88	36.54
14	20.00	19.84	—.78
15	40.00	66.78	40.10
16	75.00	307.74	75.62
17	100.00	2016.32	95.04
18	100.00	19987.86	99.49
19	100.00	336613.66	99.97
20	100.00	12823377.46	99.99 +

Some Proposals

The casinos have recently been petitioning the Gaming Control Board to raise their limits so that they can be more competitive with slots. Some want to offer $100,000 as the top prize. Others want no limit on the top end, just as there seems to be no limit on the top slot prize. They propose an increase in the prize each time someone hits a big winner.

(I would suggest just the other way around, a percentage of each bet on a particular ticket added to a progressive jackpot. Smart players could then tell when a particular ticket offered them an advantage. Just as sometimes happens on progressive slots, there would be the interesting situation of both house and player having a positive expectation.)

Opponents to raising the limits claim that the small casinos could not compete, and would be driven out of business. I don't think so. The smaller casinos devoted exclusively or primarily to slot machines do not offer $1,000,000 for a single pull of the handle, yet many of them are crowded all the time. Why? Lots of small payoffs, lots of noise, and hordes of happy players attract business. (Many of them don't even *have* keno games.) Let the casinos offer liberally-paying keno games, with high limits, and you'll see much more keno play. I suggest they even post their edge, just as many casinos now post the edge on the slot machines. (They don't phrase it that way. They speak of the percentage "return." But subtract the return from 100% to get the edge.)

I'm afraid that if the casinos get the go-ahead on the higher limits, they will also use that as an occasion to further increase their edge. (Remember when the wine manufacturers switched to metric? Similar-sized bottles at lower prices made it look like the prices had been lowered, but they were counting on the ignorance of most wine drinkers, who found it difficult to convert between price per fifth, ounce, cc, etc. In the confusion, the wineries actually *raised* their *per unit* prices.) If keno players boycott the game until the casinos give a reasonable return, the casinos may be forced to offer tickets that give the players a better gamble.

Table 1-1 also has a few suggestions for more liberal keno tickets (labeled "Proposed"). Some are bottom-weighted, giving relatively more small returns; others are top-weighted, giving relatively more large returns. I also anticipate the $100,000 limit, which I think the casinos will get. In case they ever get permission for "no-limit" keno, I've included a few suggestions for "super" payoffs. All of these could attract a lot more business, and make keno a better deal for the smart player.

Chapter 2

Blackjack Martinique Style

by Hal Straus

Catamarans coasting over calm Caribbean waters, topless sunbathers turning the glances of pot-bellied tourists, giggling children romping gleefully in the surf—some typical sights and sounds of the French Caribbean isle of Martinique.

Not the kind of place you would expect to find a hotbed of gambling fever? True enough. Among the two dozen or so Caribbean islands, Martinique is not renowned for its casinos; that distinction usually goes to Aruba, St. Maarten, or Puerto Rico, Curacao, Haiti and the Bahamas. But take heed: what the island lacks in numbers it more than compensates for with nuance.

Take the quaint yet elegant Hotel Meridien casino in the town of Pointe du Bout. Sporting only six blackjack and two craps tables, its intimate amenities—a plush, creole decor, a private bar that caters to tastes ranging from straight scotch to passion cocktails, a crew of polite, efficient dealers—can be conducive to a relaxed evening of profitable gambling.

Particularly if the gambler's game happens to be blackjack. Most nights during the off-season (August-November), you can purchase your planter's punch, plant yourself at a table, and play head-to-head with the dealer for hours—with no limit on the number of hands you can play simultaneously. Conditions are also favorable for the budget bettor: minimum wagers are ten francs (about $1.50) per hand, even for simultaneous-hand play.

Once the game begins, the play follows traditional Nevada rules—with a few very important differences. For starters, mid-deck reshuffling is strictly taboo. The cards are dealt from a four-deck shoe that is apparently invulnerable to even the most loyal dealer's manipulatory fingers or guesstimates on player-advantage situations. Frequently during the course of an evening's play, hands are interrupted so the dealer can shuffle when the shoe shows up empty.

Split-betting on pairs is handled exactly the same way as in American casinos, but doubling down is allowed for holdings of 9, 10, or 11—the 9-option providing a definite player advantage not often encountered in American casinos.

Perhaps the strangest idiosyncrasy of the Martinique game is the order in which cards are dealt—the dealer may not take his hole card until all hands have been dealt and acted upon. It should not require too much time for the skillful card counter to realize that with this rule he can "play" the dealer's hand as well as his own. In the case of a ten- or ace-rich shoe, for example, the counter playing three or four hands simultaneously (or a few players working as a team) can strip the shoe of both cards before the dealer has a shot at them.

The rule also makes the Martinique "assurance" (insurance) wager virtually senseless. The amount of the bet (half the original) and the payoff (2-1) are the same as in the U.S., but because the dealer does not get his hole card until after all other hands are played, the dealer's chances for blackjack can be substantially reduced with correct player strategy.

Believe it or not, Martinique casinos actually charge an entry fee at the door, currently 35 francs (about $5), but it can be quickly rebated at the tables with just a little luck. Besides his wallet, the gambler should also carry his passport and other identification on casino nights; the security measures at the door, apparently instituted to discourage locals, are strict and well-enforced.

Though the hot Caribbean sun and gambling are year-round industries in Martinique, the best time to travel financially speaking is during the late summer and early fall. The special airline tour packages, offering round-trip airfare from the Northeast, one week's stay in a quality hotel (breakfast included) for under $400, should be investigated. You could be in for an enjoyable, sun-filled vacation, and, if you play your cards right, a very inexpensive one.

Chapter 3

Video Poker Strategy

by Mike Caro

Andrew sat down to play video poker on my home computer. He punched in a $5 bet and the first hand he got was...

"This isn't going to be my day," said he. Telling my computer to throw away everything, he waited four-tenths of a second until the screen gobbled up the cards and replaced them with Eight-Four of Clubs, Five of Spades and Six-Seven of Diamonds. The computer chimed merrily for several seconds and announced a Straight. It paid him $20 (a $15 profit) and prompted him to wager again.

"All right!" he gloated.

But "All right" was not an appropriate remark, because all was not *right*. Oh, sure, the computer program was functioning perfectly and the weather was mild and I'd had a good day at poker. Still, a tingle rode up my spine as I realized that a lot of people would have drawn exactly the way Andrew had—five cards.

And, yet, this was terribly, hopelessly, tragically wrong! Imagine

23

the chagrin, the utter shock to the spirit, had Andrew realized what manner of blunder he had committed! Here was a fairly skilled poker player and you'd think he'd know enough to draw four. But again, maybe it was understandable, because poker players never need face that decision in normal poker.

You see, video poker is a lot different than the customary kind of poker. You don't raise, bluff or use psychology. And you play *every* hand! If this sounds like there's no skill to it, guess again. These machines are all over the casino.

I watched Andy challenge the machine I had turned my computer into. It was a fully functioning video poker machine that played and paid exactly like the progressive jackpot poker machines in Vegas.

Sidetracked

It had been devised in conjunction with *Gambling Times,* for the sole purpose of writing this chapter. Its primary function was to analyze various draws, finding whether it is better, say, to draw two to a pair of Queens or throw away a Queen and draw one to a Straight Flush. Most of these things can be done better with just a calculator and an understanding of probability, but there are some strategies that I wanted to let the computer try out while I slept.

Somewhere along the road, I'd gotten sidetracked, and the program was being used mostly as a game with the color graphics I'd added. My machine does lots more than the video machines in Las Vegas. It investigates, keeps track of your winnings, analyzes your results, allows you to select the speed of the deal and even provides an instant replay of the last hand on request.

But with folks coming over to try it out, I kept thinking my scientific program had somehow been demoted in status to an entertainment device.

Oh well, so be it...Andrew had just drawn three cards to a Queen-Jack of Hearts. He caught garbage. "Poor Andy!" said the computer.

This wasn't all wasted time for me. I watched four people play my machine this past week. What astounds me is that the same mistakes kept occurring over and over.

I guess I'd better tell you how to play right. After all, we're friends, aren't we? This chapter deals specifically with one machine—a *progressive jackpot machine* of a standard type found in Las Vegas.

Here's how it works.

You put in from one to five coins, usually quarters. The computer deals a five-card poker hand on a video screen. By pressing buttons you instruct the computer to either hold a card or throw it away. You can keep all your cards or throw away as many as you want. The machine then replaces the cards you hate, frequently with some you hate even more.

"Progressive" means that the jackpot keeps growing as more bets are made. Sometimes jackpots get very large—over $10,000. So, what must you do to win? A Royal Flush will do the trick. That's not quite as difficult as it seems, because you play every hand and you can draw to a Straight Flush instead of some other combination whenever you think it's wise.

Now, I'm going to give some straight advice, dazzle you with some figures and set you loose on the casinos with a favorable expectation.

Good thing you've got me for a friend.

David Sklansky

Speaking of friends, David Sklansky wrote a tentative report on video poker not long ago. It appeared in volume #15 of *Casino and Sports,* published by Gambler's Book Club. As always, David's insights and the quality of his research were monumental. In this chapter, I will take you even beyond David's pioneering work.

There are many varieties of poker machines, paying different amounts. The one under discussion is among the most liberal and most popular. Here's what it pays:

	(Jackpot for five coins)
Royal Flush	250 for 1
Straight Flush	50 for 1
Four of a Kind	25 for 1
Full House	8 for 1
Flush	5 for 1
Straight	4 for 1
Three of a Kind	3 for 1
Two Pair	2 for 1
Jacks, Queens Kings, Aces	1 for 1

(You get your bet back)

Try to find a machine that gives these payoffs. Remember, you're not eligible for the jackpot unless you bet the maximum—five coins. This means $1.25 on the most popular quarter machines.

So...

Video Poker Rule #1: Always bet five coins.

You will improve your chances dramatically by drawing correctly to your hands. Seemingly innocuous mistakes can, in fact, be very costly in the long run. And, keep in mind, a one-cent or two-cent error in strategy will amount to a lot in a hurry. If you're used to playing home poker at a pace of 30 hands an hour, forget it. You can play so fast your fingers will whimper!

As you probably realize, there's another element to winning besides drawing correctly, and that's finding a machine with a big enough jackpot.

According to David, $3000 is about the break-even point for a quarter machine. That means a jackpot of 2400 for 1, $12,000 on a dollar machine.

Video Poker Rule #2: Find the biggest jackpot you can.

It's a mistake to look for a lucky machine. If you see one slapping down lots of Full Houses, that doesn't mean it's in a "cycle." The machines are not programmed for cycles, they are programmed to give a fair shuffle, which, by the way, is a lot more thorough than any human shuffle. Or, at least, it is on my computer.

The first thing you should know... Let me take that back. You don't really need to know this at all, but it's interesting. The first question of interest is: *How much would an ape lose playing this machine?* Or, *How much would you lose if you were playing blindfolded?*

Turns out I have an answer to that question. If the jackpot is the recommended minimum size ($3000), then you will lose two-thirds of your money (getting 33.592 cents back for every dollar you bet). That figure is pretty stable even for a small jackpot (it begins at $1000 every time the previous one is claimed).

The computer game is only risking the $1000 it originally put into the jackpot. All additions to the jackpot come out of the players' wagers. If you decided in advance that you were going to stand pat on every hand, your mathematical return would be $1 for every $3 bet.

All right, that's the *worst* we can do. Let's improve on it.

Video Poker Rule #3: Never keep a kicker.

Let's say you've put your money in a machine and got dealt this hand...

Veteran poker players invariably consider drawing two, discarding the Eight and Six.

Whenever poker is played correctly anywhere in the Milky Way, you've got to have a *reason* to keep a kicker. What would be your reason here? Could make Aces-up, you say? True, but Aces-up is no better than Kings-up. In video poker, two pair is two pair, and Sixes and Fours is just the same as Aces and Queens. While watching my friends play my machine, I was surprised at how many kickers were kept.

Reason it out. If you draw three to Kings, what's the worst thing that could happen on the first card you catch? It could be a deuce, right? Wrong! The worst thing would be if it were of the rank you threw away. That would mean your hopes of pairing that card would be only two-thirds as good as if you'd caught a card such as a Ten. So you *could* be slightly worse off by not keeping the Ace kicker. But the difference is negligible.

The thing that's terrific about *not* keeping the kicker is that you have a nearly 50% better chance of catching a third King. And that pays 3 for 1. Remember Video Poker Rule #1 applies to Three-of-a-Kind, also.

As my friends tried out my machine, they wrote down hands that gave them problems. One that was listed by three out of the four players was this . . . Is it better to draw three cards to a Royal, keeping a Ten, or four to a face card?

Here's an illustration . . .

By the way, don't even consider drawing two to the small straight. Your choice is four to the Jack of Hearts or three to the Jack-Ten of Hearts.

What would you do? The thing to keep in mind is that far more money is paid out by the machine for one pair of Jacks, Queens, Kings or Aces than for any other kind of hand. So by throwing the Ten away, you get an extra shot at making a pair of Jacks. On the other hand you sacrifice your shot at the jackpot, because you can no longer make a Royal Flush.

Hey, Mike, could you tell me approximately how hard it is to make that three-card Royal? Sure, I'll do better than that. . . I'll tell you *exactly* how hard it is. It's a 16,241 to 1 against it. So it seems that this chance might be too remote to merit keeping the Ten. But is it? There's only one way to know for sure. It's to find out just how much you'll get back for a dollar's worth of bet if you draw three. And how much if you draw four.

This is the breakdown:

If you draw four to the Jack of Diamonds. . .

(178,365 possible combinations of cards)

Hand Made	Winning Combinations	Penny Value
Royal Flush	0	0.00
Straight Flush	0	0.00
Four of a Kind	52	0.73
Full House	216	0.97
Flush	330	0.93
Straight	832	1.87
Three of a Kind	4,102	6.90
Two Pair	8,874	9.95
Pair Jacks. . . Aces	45,456	25.49

Value: 46.8 cents.

Now, what if you draw only three cards, keeping the Jack-Ten of Diamonds?

Hand Made	Winning Combinations	Penny Value
Royal Flush	1	14.80
Straight Flush	3	0.93
Four of a Kind	2	0.31
Full House	18	0.89
Flush	161	4.97
Straight	252	6.22
Three of a Kind	281	5.20
Two Pair	711	8.77
Pair Jacks...Aces	2,955	18.22

Value: 60.3 cents.

Just like that we've learned it's much better to keep the Ten and draw three to the Royal. This shows you a means of itemizing all possible results and determining the correct strategy. You see, it isn't guesswork; it's science. The manner in which these combinations of hands were derived is beyond the scope of this chapter. However, the same precise method was used in formulating this overall strategy.

In this previous example, it's important to point out that this particular four-card draw was handicapped *because* the suited Ten was discarded. Normally a four-card draw to a Jack returns about 48%, depending on the ranks and suits of the discards.

So...

Video Poker Rule #4: Never draw four if you can draw three to a Royal.

If you have a hand like...

you could think about drawing four to the Queen. Certainly that's better than drawing four to the damaged Jack. But, still, it's better to draw to the Royal, even if the jackpot is only $1000 (in which case you shouldn't be playing). You might consider drawing two, but that's also wrong.

Now look at this...

Forget about drawing two to the Flush. That's a real loser. The question is, should you draw two cards or three cards in this case? If you drew two, which cards would you keep? The answer is keep the Queen and Jack because the Straight opportunities for King and Queen are fewer (because it's more dead-ended on the high side).

(By the way, for the above reason, a four-card draw to a Jack is slightly better than a four-card draw to a Queen. And Kings and Aces are still worse—though equally so.)

It happens that the answer to the previous problem is to draw only two. That returns 51% as compared to 49% for a three-card draw.

Video Poker Rule #5: Don't break a Flush to draw one to a Straight Flush.

This is a common mistake.

Here's your hand...

The pat hand is already worth a 500% return. That is, your original $1.25 and an additional $5.00. So right now you're getting back $6.25. How much comes back if you draw?

You'd get $2.66 worth of Straight Flush, 80 cents worth of ordinary Flush and 8 cents worth of Jacks. We're talking about $3.54 here; and we're paying $6.25 to draw. You see, that one isn't even close!

And for the same reason, though not quite as compelling...

Video Poker Rule #6: Never break a Straight to draw to a Straight Flush.

Of course, a video poker machine does not consider a Royal Flush to be the same thing as a Straight Flush. If it's a Royal we're talking about, then that's completely different. In fact...

Video Poker Rule #7: Always break a Flush to draw to a Royal.

Video Poker Rule #8: Always break a Straight to draw to a Royal.

These last two rules imply something so obvious I won't bother to make a rule out of it: *Always break a pair to draw to a Royal.*

But this isn't so obvious...

Video Poker Rule #9: Always break anything to draw to a Royal. (This assumes the jackpot is David's minimum $3000 or higher for a quarter machine.)

It is my opinion that you can beat a machine with a jackpot even smaller than $3000, but I'm not sure yet.

It's important to realize that there is a theoretical time when the jackpot gets so big that you would break any hand and draw like crazy. For instance, if the jackpot were $20,000,000, that's big enough to throw away a pat 9-high Straight Flush and draw five. No, $19,000,000 is *not* big enough! There's a point at which you'd have to break any hand, but in actual practice, you won't have to worry about it. Meanwhile, use this strategy which works even better as the jackpot increases beyond $3000.

Video Poker Rule #10: Never draw five if you have any card larger than a Ten.

Remember Andrew at the beginning of this article? He violated this rule and look where it got him. (He made a Straight!) Well, it's right in the long run, I promise.

Video Poker Rule #11: Don't keep a Ten for a four-card draw.

These rules and the related advice given are not intended to cover all aspects of video poker. A discussion of each dilemma you're apt to face would require a book-length volume. Some research is still not complete.

One last rundown of statistics before I give you my easy-to-use system.

Let's say the jackpot is $3000 for your $1.25 bet. What is it worth to you to be drawing one to a Royal Flush? It turns out there are three different Royals you can draw to ranging in return-per-dollar from $52.36 to $53.57. The best one you can hope for is King-Queen-Jack-Ten. The average of these three types is $52.79 per dollar, and on your $1.25 bet that means the value of your situation before you draw is $65.99. Therefore, if someone sneaks up behind you and offers $50 to take over your hand, you should not sell it.

It occurs to me money could be made by approaching players and offering to buy hands before the draw. In that light, here are some interesting stats.

With five quarters already invested:

A one-card draw to an open-end Straight Flush is worth $4.23, plus 8 cents for every card higher than a Ten.

A one-card draw to an inside Straight Flush is worth $2.71, plus 8 cents for every card higher than a Ten.

A one-card draw to a Flush is worth $1.20, plus 8 cents for every card higher than a Ten.

A one-card draw to an open-end Straight is worth 85 cents plus 8 cents for every card higher than a Ten.

A one-card draw to an inside Straight is worth 43 cents (rounded off—it's actually worth exactly half an open-end Straight) plus 8 cents for every card higher than a Ten.

This last item is fairly interesting. It means that if you hold...

you will get 75 cents back out of your $1.25 on average if you draw one. Earlier in this chapter you learned that a two-card draw to three high cards was better than either a three-card or a four-card draw. The two-card draw, remember, returns 51%. On a $1.25 wager, that comes to only 64 cents. It's clearly better to draw one.

However, if two of these four high cards are suited (and they will be 91% of the time), you should draw three to the Royal. (That is, unless the jackpot is not much above our recommended minimum of $3000.)

Here's what your hand is worth for a $1.25 bet on some other draws:

A two-card draw to Three-of-a-Kind is worth $5.57; three to a pair of Jacks, $2.30; three to a pair of Sixes, $1.41.

A two-card draw to King-Queen-Jack is worth 64 cents. Note that drawing to Ace-King-Queen is not as good due to diminished Straight possibilities. (In fact, it's only worth 56 cents.) Still it's better to draw two than three, unless two of these cards are suited.

A two-card draw to a Flush is only worth 38 cents whereas a five-card draw is worth about 45 cents. I'm not sure of the precision of this last figure. It depends on which cards you throw away. Once you've thrown away five garbage cards, your chances of snatching something worthwhile are better than from a full deck of 52 cards. Don't forget, right now the return we're dealing with is per $1.25. A *return-per-dollar* on a five-card draw is only about 36 cents.

If you'd rather deal in dollars altogether, convert the figures on this list by dividing by 5 and then multiplying by 4.

For your $1.25, a two-card Straight draw like 9-8-7, discarding 4-2, is worth 34 cents. Obviously, you should draw five instead. Three cards to Queen-Jack returns 64 cents; to King-Queen or King-Jack, 62 cents; to Ace-King, Ace-Queen or Ace-Jack, 60 cents.

A four-card draw to a Jack returns 60 cents (and varies slightly depending on your discards; throwing a suited Ten brings it down 1.8 cents). Four to an Ace or King is worth 59 cents and four to a Queen is in between.

Now let's take this information and make it win.

In Table 3-1, you'll find my *Baby Steps for Best Profit*. Take it to the casino if you want. As you get familiar with the routine, the procedure will become automatic. I'm assuming the jackpot is 2400 times the sum of your five coins ($3000 on a quarter machine). Do exactly as instructed.

Table 3-1

Mike Caro's
BABY STEPS FOR BEST PROFIT

(Quarter machine with $3000 jackpot.)

If you don't want to play a hand then quit
Otherwise continue
Insert five coins and play

"GLORY GROVE"

If you have a Royal Flush then stand pat and start over
Otherwise continue
If you have four cards of a Royal Flush then draw one
and start over
(Even if this means breaking up a King-high Straight
Flush)
Otherwise continue
If you have a Straight then stand pat and start over
Otherwise continue
If you have at least four of the same suit then skip to
"Garden of One Color"
Otherwise continue
If you have any paired cards then skip to "Land of
Companions"
Otherwise continue

"LONGSHOT LOBBY"

If you have three cards of a Royal Flush then draw two
and start over

Otherwise continue

If you have an open-end Straight opportunity then draw one and start over
Otherwise continue

If you have two cards of a Royal Flush then draw three and start over
Otherwise continue

If you have King-Queen-Jack then draw two and start over
Otherwise continue

If you have two cards higher than a Ten then draw three and start over
Otherwise continue

If you have a card higher than a Ten then draw four and start over
Otherwise continue

If you have three cards of a Straight Flush then draw two and start over
Otherwise continue

Draw five and start over

"GARDEN OF ONE COLOR"

If you have a Flush then stand pat and start over
Otherwise continue

If you have three cards of a Royal Flush then draw two and start over
Otherwise continue

If you have four cards of a Straight Flush then draw one and start over
Otherwise continue

If you have a pair higher than Tens then draw three and start over
Otherwise continue

Draw one to your Flush and start over

"LAND OF COMPANIONS"

If you have Four-of-a-Kind or a Full House then stand
pat and start over
Otherwise continue
If you have Three-of-a-Kind then draw two and start over
Otherwise continue
If you have three cards of a Royal Flush then draw two
and start over
Otherwise continue
If you have two pair then draw one and start over
Otherwise continue
Draw three to your pair and start over

You can try this strategy on quarter-machine jackpots ranging from $2500 to $5000, but you'll have to shop around. Some categories of hands have been lumped together even though the return varies. Example: Drawing to 9-8-7 suited returns about 60%, but 9-8-5 suited returns just about 40%. Due to their rarity, I call them both two-card draws to Straight Flushes. Nevertheless, if you follow these "Baby Steps" exactly, you will NEVER make a significant mistake. Finally, when the "Steps" say to draw, you will sometimes need to make obvious choices. For instance, if you have two 3-card Royal draws, K-Q and J-10, you would keep the K-Q.

Poker Terminology

BLUFF—The ability to misrepresent one's hand.

DRAW—The basic style of poker in which each player is dealt five cards, face down.

FLUSH—Any five cards, all of the same suit.

FOUR OF A KIND—Any four cards of the same denomination, i.e., four Queens, four Nines, etc.

FULL HOUSE—A hand with three of a kind and two of a kind, of any denomination.

ROYAL FLUSH—The Ten, Jack, Queen, King and Ace of one suit. This is poker's top hand.

STRAIGHT—Five cards of any suit, in sequence.

STRAIGHT FLUSH—Five cards of the same suit in sequence.

TRIPS—Three of a kind.

Section Two
SPORTS BETTING

Whether your game is football, jai alai, or dog racing, the following five chapters provide insight into the sports and the methods the pros use to make them profitable.

Section Two
SPORTS BETTING

Chapter 4

Beating the Pointspread

by Stan Shapiro

The relationship between the linemaker and the pointspread is a good place to begin this chapter because most bettors think the linemaker has designed the betting line to beat them out of their money. Actually, nothing is further from the truth. The "line" is simply a neutral beginning for two opposing bettors.

In Las Vegas, all bettors lay $11 to win $10. Therefore, if half the bettors like Team A and the other half like Team B, exactly one half will lose $11 and the other half will collect $10. That lopsided difference of $1 from each bettor on the losing side is known as the vigorish (sometimes referred to as "the vig") or the juice.

Essentially, this difference is the amount kept by the sports book for holding the money. Any adjustment in the betting line is merely an attempt by the book to keep a perfect balance between the two betting sides.

The foregoing enables us to view the pointspread without presumptuous bias and, knowing this, we can get off to a good start by simply realizing that the pointspread represents the opinion of exactly one-half the bettors at any given time, the winners and the losers! The trick is to get on the winning side.

"Don't pick the winner." This is an interesting concept because most people are win-oriented and therefore preoccupied with who will win. But, in my opinion, football games are not won, they are lost. I'll have more to say on this concept as we go along.

Eight basic factors determine the outcome of every football meeting. They are the schedule, the weather, injuries, emotions, the turf, the kicking game, the turnovers, and the coaches.

Perhaps 90% of all wagers in sports are made emotionally, without regard to all eight of the basic factors. Assuming 10% of the bettors considered one or two of the basic factors involved, I'd say 99% are still making a guess as to which team will win. After all, with no more than 25% of the homework completed, how much can they know?

Fortunately for us, the pointspread has divided the bettors into two camps but, basically, for either side, the loser could be determined by the toss of a coin. We all have access to the same information, but if we all analyzed the game the same way, the pointspread would be drastically different. Therefore, the pointspread doesn't determine the outcome of the game—the losers do.

Analyzing the Eight Basic Factors

(1) *The schedule*—The teams do not all play each other—they can't. There are 28 teams, each playing only 16 games (eight on the road and eight at home). While some of the games appear to be easy, any coach will tell you what a tough schedule can do to break a good team down.

Conversely, an easy schedule will tend to make a poor team look good. Regardless of how tough their schedule may be, we're concerned with performance against the betting line and that has to be measured from week to week as the season progresses.

(2) *The weather*—Unlike baseball, once the football season begins, that's it. Nothing—not wind, not rain, not even snow—will interfere with a scheduled football game. And to a veteran handicapper, these elements can play an important role in the outcome of a crucial game. Put some of our born-and-raised California boys on a field in Denver, up to their ankles in snow around the 13th week of the season in November, and I'll show you what a *real* Thanksgiving Day "turkey" looks like!

In inclement weather I look for two things: coaching and

special teams. The better coach has the ability to spot a weakness in the opponent's defense and can capitalize on it quickly. Under adverse conditions, ball control is absolutely essential. Well-coached teams can stop a ground game dead in its tracks. The following game between Buffalo (coach Chuck Knox) and New England (coach Ron Erhardt) illustrates these two points pretty well.

In the eighth week of the 1980 season, Buffalo needed a win over New England to tie for first place in the AFC East. Amidst 40 m.p.h. winds at Rich stadium in Orchard Park, neither team managed to score while facing the wind. With the wind at their backs in the first quarter, New England scored three points on a 41-yard field goal by John Smith. A mere 12-yard punt into the wind by Buffalo's punter, Greg Cater, left New England with pretty good field position. However, they failed to fully capitalize on it owing to the efforts of the Bills' strong team on defense.

Likewise, in the fourth quarter, New England punter Mike Hubach, a rookie out of Kansas, laid one out only eight yards, allowing Buffalo to score seven points on a short drive to the end zone.

All in all, I'd say the wind played an important part in putting New England's balls all over the field as the Bills intercepted four Grogan passes and then held them to just 39 yards, rushing to win the game 31-13.

Following the game, Buffalo coach Chuck Knox, who thoroughly outcoached New England's Ron Erhardt, said, "You had to be on the field to appreciate how bad it [the wind] was." The statistics in this game clearly point out what a factor the weather can be.

New England	3 —	0 —	10 —	0 —	13
Buffalo	0 —	14 —	0 —	17 —	31

	New England	3
1st Quarter	Buffalo	0

Buffalo's strong defense held New England at mid-field, forcing them to try a 41-yard field goal. They made it because the wind was blowing in their favor and carried the ball a great distance. Buffalo could not capitalize with the wind against them.

	New England	0
2nd Quarter	Buffalo	14

Buffalo scored seven points twice, pointing out a weak New England defense. (Remember games are not *won,* they are *lost.*) Against the wind, New England could not score. (In just two quarters of play, the weaker team made itself apparent.)

By half-time we've learned that: Buffalo has a strong defense; New England has a weak defense; the wind is a definite factor, making it virtually impossible for either team to get off long kicks against it; Buffalo has a better coach with a great deal more strategic experience; and Buffalo makes a great second-half bet when you only had to lay three points to get them.

	New England	10
3rd Quarter	Buffalo	0

Again, the stiff wind kept New England close to the goal, allowing them to score seven points only once. A strong Buffalo defense allowed only a field goal on the second try. Buffalo could not score against the wind.

	New England	0
4th Quarter	Buffalo	17

Here in the final quarter, the full story is told. Neither team can score against 40 m.p.h. winds. New England, the weaker of the two teams, could not keep Buffalo from scoring seven points twice. And for good measure, they politely allowed a field goal and bowed out!

Without getting emotional, those of us who bothered to learn the weather conditions at Rich Stadium on the day of the game had a decisive edge. Forty m.p.h. winds indicate that at least 50% of the game will be played on the ground. Punts of eight or ten yards against the wind are expected and, therefore, a good defense for virtually goal-line stands will be mandatory.

These factors, combined with New England's poor defense and Buffalo's far more experienced coaching staff, provided the knowledgeable bettor with a first-rate bet twice in the same game.

(3) *Injuries*—This is one of the toughest areas to assess in handicapping. Even though the information provided by the press is complete and available to everyone, an injury is only signficant if the team cannot fill the vacant position with a comparable player.

Analyzing team depth can be difficult and for this I rely on draft reports and college performances available in weekly papers like *College and Pro Football Newsweekly* or *H&H Sporting Times,* which I save for years in rooms full of files. A good coach understands the importance of attacking a key position when he knows there is no real back-up threat. Here's an example for the way I evaluate injuries:

St. Louis quarterback Jim Hart was sacked six times in the seventh week of the 1980 season by the Washington Redskins, who shut them down 23-0. Does this mean St. Louis has a weak offensive line? You bet it does! Any time the QB is continuously sacked the line is to blame, and if it goes unchanged you can expect a serious injury.

In St. Louis' case, weaknesses are blatant; one only has to review their draft to spot them. In the first six rounds alone, they drafted three linebackers and a quarterback. (I can't help but think they drafted the quarterback knowing that Jim Hart was on a kamikaze mission and eventually would be seriously hurt.)

So, for me, evalualting injuries becomes a two-step process:

49

one in which I'm looking at the draft to spot an overall weakness in the team, and one in which I'm reviewing scouting reports and newspaper statistics to evaluate the quality of those players drafted. This way, when something happens to a key player, I know in advance just how seriously this will affect the overall performance of the team. You may even be surprised at how often a team will play better with a replacement for a key man.

(4) *Emotions*—Of all the factors involved in the selection process, this is by far the most interesting. It is also undoubtedly the single most important element taken into consideration by serious professional gamblers in deciding the outcome of any football game.

That old cliche, "Win one for the Gipper," still rings true, and while Hollywood may dwell on fantasy and sentiment, it is a well-known fact that if you can get those overgrown boys "up" for the game they'll move mountains to come back victorious.

Interesting as it is, though, I've found it nearly impossible to second guess this strange phenomenon. At best, one stands only a 50% chance of being correct when it comes to "guessing" what a team feels like before the big game.

So, if emotions play such an important role in the outcome and you've got a 50% chance of being correct about them, how, you may ask, can you possibly evaluate the intangibles with any degree of accuracy? Well, it's actually quite simple.

Earlier, you will recall, I stated, "Don't pick the winner," and to illustrate my point with regard to emotions let's go back to the 14th week of the season in 1980 when the Green Bay Packers went off to Chicago to take on the Bears. In that game Chicago scored its biggest victory in 15 years as they humiliated the Packers in front of 57,176 blood-thirsty fans in a 61-7 annihilation. According to Chicago quarterback Vince Evans, the Packers had it coming to them for the heartbreak they caused in the season opener when Green Bay won 12-6, as the Packer's FG kicker Chester Marcol scored a touchdown after his field goal attempt in overtime was blocked and, surprisingly, the ball bounced back into his arms.

Indeed, a serendipitous turn of events for Green Bay who, up to that point, had not celebrated a single touchdown in the previous four games. Getting even for embarrassing moments certainly weighs heavily on the emotional scale of football and, if all goes true to form, it's a certainty the Packers will return to avenge this incredible nightmare.

(5) *The turf*—Certainly all football players have a variety of shoes—some for dry grass and some for wet. Additionally, they have shoes for carpet and what is known as P.A.T.—"prescription athletic turf." There are three types of playing surfaces. It pays to know the type of surface your team will play on.

I've found that a team that continually practices on natural turf has trouble playing on artificial or P.A.T and vice versa. A visiting team used to natural grass with a low moisture content has a hell of a time trying to get a good hold on wet athletic turf.

Incidentally, some coaches are so smart they'll purposely water the lawn for a couple of days prior to a game to slow a fast team down. Great runners like Campbell for the Houston Oilers or Payton for the Chicago Bears have been brought to their knees by a few smart coaches! On the other hand, a runner used to P.A.T. in good weather can cut very sharp turns, making life miserable for the opponent. When all stadiums move indoors we can throw out two factors: the weather and the turf!

(6) *The kicking game*—If you've analyzed the opponent and you know they have a good defense, check your field goal specialist—he'd better be good. Likewise, a good punter can put the ball in a spot that keeps a ground team at bay throughout an entire game.

When it's fourth and 10 and the goal line is 90 yards away, what do you have to look forward to? Punt, and if you're on the wrong team, pray!

(7) *The turnovers*—Here's where the ball with the funny shape drives us all nuts. Imagine this, if you will: It's the fourth quarter and your team has a seven-point advantage over the opponent.

Your guys have the ball and they've just made three successive first downs and they're well on their way to the end zone. You need to win the game by only four points and there are less than five minutes left to play in the game. You're eating up the time on the clock, sipping on your beer and congratulating yourself for picking another winner.

All of a sudden your hero, "Fast Freddie" with the fancy feet, runs smack into "Freight-Train Willie," who lost his last tooth at the age of 12 when he tried teething on a fireplug and now rips them out of street corners with his bare hands in revenge. The ball pops loose and with a few of those weird dumb bounces winds up in the hands of "Speed-Ball Nelson," your most hated enemy, who carries the ball all the way back to your 20-yard line! Damn, why didn't he hold onto it? He knew "Freight-Train" was there!

Now you experience that sinking feeling. You know what I'm talking about, don't you? The light at the end of the tunnel was really an oncoming train.

Now let's see why you always lose when this happens.

First of all, you lost the ball. The fans for the other side go crazy, screaming and cheering. Your side died, period! They take off their helmets and walk off the field with their heads hanging in disgust and defeat. The other side sends in a freshly hyped-up offense who sincerely believes they'll tie this game up (and you just know they will); your side sends in a tired defense who only moments before was about to head for the showers with a victory under their belts.

You've just experienced a "turnover," a complete reversal of momentum in a game. And you know the outcome—they tie up the game! Your offense comes back, uses up some more of the clock, and finally wins the game with a lousy field goal with seven seconds remaining. What utter frustration!

Well, that's why they call it gambling. But, there are records to indicate which teams are turnover-prone and which teams actually cause turnovers. Fortunately, magazines like *College and Pro Football Weekly* and *H&H Sporting Times* keep a running account of which teams are which and a good handicapper will always glance at this record just to be aware of the potential hazard.

In case you think this might be a waste of time, remember that Tom Landry, one of the finest coaches in the country, hired a kid solely for his ability to intercept passes in *college*. Is it really a coincidence that this kid still holds the record for the most interceptions in the NFL?

You can think what you want, but I prefer to think that kid knows where the ball is going to be and I'll bet on it! Know the turnover factor—the teams with the best and worst records—because they are going to meet each other!

(8) *The coaches*—Good coaches square-off against their opponents and play the match like a chess game. There are a few things to consider when you pick the *loser*.

If you want to bet on the Dallas Cowboys, for example, bear in mind that this is considered "America's Team," and with a winning record like Tom Landry's as head coach, don't expect any bargains when it comes to the pointspread.

People's psychological preferences for a team like Dallas will cause a lopsided pointspread in the game. Not that it can't be overcome, mind you, but it can make life a bit more difficult.

Before you make a bet on any "popular" team, think in terms of the percentage of points you must lay to win the game. For example, if you are asked to lay 14½ points in a game where the linemaker estimates the total number of points in that game to be 35, then you must score on the opponent with three touchdowns for every touchdown the underdog makes. Here you are asked to lay 40% of the total production of points in the game. If your team is winning 21-0 in the fourth quarter, just how difficult is it for your team to keep from letting up?

Which coach needs to score at this point? It doesn't take a genius to know that a single touchdown by the opponent has cost you the game. My advice is to look for games which appear to be close calls with low pointspreads, do your homework by evaluating the eight basic factors, then size up the coaches against all known facts before you make your selection.

Keep in mind that some coaches, like Bum Phillips, Ray Malavasi or Don Shula, don't care what the betting line is. They are satisfied to win the game. These coaches, even if they are on the one-yard line, will freeze the ball if they're ahead by a single point with less than 25 seconds remaining. Also remember factor four—emotions—if revenge becomes a factor, the opponent will be tougher to beat the next time the teams meet.

I recall a night game played in 1980, when the Rams destroyed Dallas, 38-14, in Los Angeles. Three weeks later, during the playoffs, the Rams had the misfortune to meet up with Dallas again, but this time in Dallas and on less than friendly terms. The Rams went down hard in a devastating blood bath, a re-match they'll remember for some time to come.

It is interesting to note that Dallas' coach, Tom Landry, pointed out almost immediately following the first game that his team would be waiting for the Rams when they got to Texas in the ensuing weeks ahead. Listen to the coach—when he's angry you can bet the players are going to be tough competitors the next time around.

A Few Points for Analysis

Given the time, most of us have the ability to analyze the eight basic factors I've outlined here. I've repeatedly stressed the importance of "doing your homework" because this is the key to evaluating each and every match-up throughout the 16 weeks of the season. In fact, "homework" should be the ninth factor, because without it you'll be the loser.

Chapter 5

Hedging and Middling

by David Sklansky

One of the most widely misunderstood concepts in gambling is that of hedging bets. This is a technique that is used most commonly in sports betting, but it can come up in other gambling events. In general, hedging is usually the wrong play. There are times, however, when it isn't—simple logical analysis can tell us which times are which.

When someone hedges a bet they are, in essence, betting against themselves. They are making a second bet after an original bet where, if they win the second bet, they probably lost the first one and vice versa. It is frequently done to ensure a profit.

For example, if a player has blackjack and buys insurance against a dealer's Ace showing, he is really making a second bet (that the dealer has a Ten in the hole) that is a hedge against his first bet. By doing so he ensures a payoff of even money, rather than either getting a push or a payoff of three to two odds. Other examples of hedges are:

(1) Betting a football game one way and then, after jumping off to an early lead, betting the other way at half time;

(2) Betting the Daily Double and then betting other horses in the second race after the first horse has won;

(3) Betting a five-team football parlay and then betting the opposite team in the fifth game after your first four teams have won;

(4) Betting on a baseball team to win the pennant before the season starts and then betting against them in the divisional playoffs, and;

(5) Betting one side of a game or sporting event and then betting the other side after the odds have shifted in your favor.

Take the case of a half-time hedge in football. Suppose you originally bet the underdog getting 10½ points. Your team now jumps off to a 7-point lead at the half. The bookmaker installs the other team as a 6½-point favorite in the second half. (In Nevada it is quite common for bookmakers to put up a pointspread on the second half of a televised game.)

You reason that by laying the 6½ points, you ensure winning at least one of your bets and may very well win both. (If the original favorite outscores the original underdog by between 7 and 17 points in the second half you do, in fact, win both bets.) If not, you win either your original bet or your half-time bet. This seems like a golden opportunity to go for a 10-point "middle." In spite of the foregoing reasoning, however, making this second bet at the half is probably a bad play.

The basic principle is this: If the second bet has the worst of it, you will cost yourself money in the long run by making it. This second hedge bet is really a separate bet. Previous bets should not usually be an excuse to make a bad bet now.

Let's look at a clear-cut example of this principle from the game of craps. Suppose you bet $7 on don't pass and the shooter comes out with a point of four. You now get the idea that you can hedge your bet by placing the four for $5, getting nine-to-five odds. This ensures a $2 profit since if the four comes up before a seven you lose your $7 don't pass bet but collect $9 on your place bet.

If the seven shows before the four, you lose your $5 place bet, but win your $7 don't pass bet. Either way you show a $2 profit. The flaw in this idea is that your average profit is higher if you don't hedge. If you just let your $7 don't pass bet ride, you will win two out of three of them (when the point is four). Thus, you figure to be $7 ahead after three such decisions. This works out to about $2.67 per decision. Hedging your bet costs you an average of 67ᶜ.

Of course, hedging is correct if the second bet is a good bet by itself. Say, for example, you have won the first half of the Daily Double and now notice that a horse you don't have in the second half is going off at much higher odds than expected. You should certainly bet it if it has become a good one. It's only a coincidence that it appears to be a hedge bet; you would have bet it even if your weren't alive with another horse in the double.

One time it is acceptable to make a hedge bet purely as a hedge is when this bet is dead even. In this case you are only making the second bet because of the existence of the first bet, yet aren't costing yourself anything by doing it and are reducing your fluctuations.

There was a situation recently in Reno that almost forced you to hedge if you bet. Harolds Club had a football parlay card that was paying something like 20 for 1 on five out of five winners and 50 for 1 on six out of six. The true odds are, of course, 32 for 1 and 64 for 1, respectively.

However, let's say that because of line movements during the week you find five very good bets on the card. You still shouldn't bet a five-teamer. Rather than bet a $10 five-team parlay card, you should bet two $5 six-team cards. You do this by picking *any* game for your sixth game and going both ways on it while betting your five key games on both cards. To show you why this is better, let's say your five teams win. If you only bet one $10 card, it would be worth $200. Had you bet two $5 cards, one of the cards would lose but the other would be worth $250. Yet in spite of this, I observed many people betting five-team parlay cards though it couldn't possibly be right even if they knew the winners.

There are some situations where a good case can be made for taking the worst of it on hedge bets. They occur when you are on a limited bankroll and the knowledge of a future hedge opportunity allows you to make a bigger wager than you could otherwise afford on what you know to be a very good bet.

For instance, suppose you thought that the Cincinnati Bengals had a very good chance to win the Central Division of the AFC several seasons ago. However, the only bet available to you was on their winning the Super Bowl (you could get 100-1 in some spots). Well, even though you really only liked them to win the division, you should still take the 100-1 on the Super Bowl and then perhaps start betting *against* them in the playoffs (taking slightly the worst of it on these bets) in order to ensure a profit. This is still better than making a much smaller bet to start with because of your limited bankroll and then not hedging.

To make this principle crystal clear, take this hypothetical example from baseball. The Yankees are playing the Dodgers. One bookie has the Yankees a 1.80-1.60 favorite. You are sure the game is even money. You have a $10,000 bankroll. You can middle this game by laying 1.40 and taking 1.60 and thus make a sure profit, but this seems silly since you know laying 1.40 is a bad bet.

I've been saying in this chapter that you shouldn't make bad bets just to ensure a profit—but this is an exception. If you were to only bet the Dodgers, you could really only afford to bet about $1000 (getting $1600-$1000 odds). If the game is truly even money, this should give you an average profit of $300. However, if you bet both ways you can pull all $10,000 in action, since you can't lose.

By betting about $6025 on the Yankees and $3975 on the Dodgers, you must come out with a profit of about $330. It is important to understand that if the bookies only had a $1000 limit, or even a $3000 limit, it would have been better to bet the $1000 on the Dodgers rather than to go for the sure profit. The middle is worth it (when one side is a bad bet) only if it allows you to put far more money into action.

In the example just discussed, had you originally bet $1000 on the Dodgers (getting 1.60) and then discovered you could lay 1.40 on the Yankees, you should not do it just to ensure a profit as long as you think you can go back and bet far more on the original bet and a similar amount on the hedge bet.

To put it another way you should not try to middle a game if you had originally bet it one way just because the line has moved. That is, unless this new line means that your second bet has also become a good bet or you have the opportunity to put much more money into action.

It is especially important to understand the foregoing concepts when betting football. Suppose one bookie has the Colts a 4½-point favorite and another one has them a 7½-point favorite.

Almost all bettors would go for a middle by laying the 4½ and taking the 7½.

Suppose however, you're sure that the right line is 2. Shouldn't you just take the 7½? Don't you do better in the long run? The answer is yes only if you can afford to bet the limit.

If the bookie's limit is $2200 but can only afford to bet $550 taking the 7½ points, you're better off betting $2200 both ways. You are really only risking $200 now and stand to win $4000 if the Colts win by 5, 6, or 7. (There is another option if you are sure it's a great bet taking the 7½. Bet both ways, but bet more on the underdog. If you bet $2200 on the dog and $1650 on the favorite you still have a nice middle going for you but still show a profit if your side wins.)

In practice, if there is a three-point line discrepancy, it is likely that the true line is somewhere in the middle. Besides, most people are not good enough handicappers to judge the true line. The discrepancy has to give you the best of it—so go for it.

Chapter 6

Pro Football's Ten Greatest Betting Systems

by Ernie Kaufman

The recent "coming out of the closet" of sports gambling has prompted hundreds of national publications to carry gambling-related articles on their pages. Within this media barrage one finds daily pointspreads, assorted handicappers' opinions, and a massive dose of "how-to-handicap" systems specifically geared to the sports bettor. With the whole world writing and/or publishing handicapping aids, one gets the impression that reliable handicapping systems are a dime a dozen.

Unfortunately, that is not the case. The majority of the published sports handicapping information is virtually useless. The information is usually inaccurate, the systems are not logical, and the methods do not go back far enough into previous seasons to confirm their validity.

Those who have read my articles in *Gambling Times* know the main thrust of my personal handicapping method is the use of reliable systems. So what I have done is extract, from the hundreds of systems that I work with in my handicapping, the ten pro football systems that I believe to be the most reliable.

System #1—Bet against any pro football team that is playing a third consecutive road game. *Pointspread results:* 29 wins and 13 losses—or 69% winning bets over four football seasons.

System #2—Bet on any intra-division pro football *home* team that is either a pointspread underdog, or "pick 'em" or a small favorite that is giving no more than one point. (Intra-division games are games played between teams in the same division. Examples are Dallas against Philadelphia, Los Angeles against San Francisco, Chicago against Minnesota, etc.) *Pointspread results:* 199 wins and 98 losses—or 67% winning bets over eight football seasons.

System #3—Bet on any home team that has scored 20 or less points in their previous three games to cover the pointspread. *Pointspread results:* 42 wins and 23 losses—or 65% winning bets over four football seasons.

System #4—Bet on any road underdog that is receiving 7½ or more points during the first four weeks of any new football season. *Pointspread results:* 23 winners and eight losses—or 74% winning bets over four football seasons.

System #5—Bet on any team, home or away, that has scored seven or less points in each of their last two games. *Pointspread results:* 33 winners and 12 losers—or 73% winning bets over eight football seasons.

System #6—Bet on any *home* team to cover the points if they have failed to cover in each of their last three games. *Pointspread results:* 67 winners and 36 losses—65% winning bets over eight football seasons.

System #7—Bet on any home team underdogs to cover the pointspread. *Pointspread results:* 166 winners and 104 losses—or 61% winning bets over four football seasons.

System #8—Bet on any home team underdog that has scored 10 or less points in their previous game. *Pointspread results:* 116 winners and 52 losses—or 69% winning bets over eight football seasons.

System #9—Bet against last year's "Super Bowl" winner in their second, third, fourth, and fifth games of the new season. *Pointspread results:* 28 winners and 12 losses—or 70% winning bets over ten football seasons.

System #10—Bet against any road team that is a pointspread favorite while they are changing playing surfaces from natural grass to astro-turf. *Pointspread results:* 95 winners and 46 losses—or 67% winning bets over eight football seasons.

(NFL teams whose playing surface is natural grass are the Atlanta Falcons, Baltimore Colts, Cleveland Browns, Denver Broncos, Green Bay Packers, Kansas City Chiefs, Los Angeles Rams, Miami Dolphins, New York Jets, Los Angeles Raiders, San Diego Chargers, San Francisco 49ers, Tampa Bay Bucs, and Washington Redskins.

Those whose playing surface is astro-turf are the Buffalo Bills, Chicago Bears, Cincinnati Bengals, Dallas Cowboys, Detroit Lions, Houston Oilers, Minnesota Vikings, New England Patriots, New Orleans Saints, New York Giants, Pittsburgh Steelers, Philadelphia Eagles, Seattle Seahawks, and St. Louis Cardinals.)

If normal probabilities occur, then at least six, and maybe seven, of these systems will demonstrate a profit in future seasons. Bet on it!

Chapter 7

Upgraded Dogs Up the Profits

by Ross Hamilton

There is more misconception surrounding the sport of dog racing than any other form of racing. There is an almost unlimited supply of literature involving the activities of both standardbreds and thoroughbreds, but when it comes to the greyhounds the cupboard is nearly bare. For the past two decades, Jack Fink has written knowledgeably about the pups in his weekly column in the *Miami Racing Record*. In all fairness, however, I must add that Jack didn't like to stick his neck out or venture far out on a canine limb. He much preferred generalities. Sensing this need for factual help for the neophyte greyhound handicapper, I tried to fill this void with my book, *Greyhound Betting for Profit*.

Dogs moving up or down the class ladder had always interested handicappers. Coming down in class has characteristically drawn the most attention. Everything else being equal, it is safe to say that the animal moving down will go off at a short price. In the case of greyhounds, an entry who runs out of the money in his three previous starts, regardless of bumps, bad boxes or poor racing luck, drops one racing grade.

Generally speaking, a grade drop is a plus factor and should not be ignored in assessing the race. If, however, a dog drops from three favorable boxes (1-2-3 or 8) into an undesirable 4, 5, 6 or 7 hole, this plus factor loses most of its luster. Another minus feature concerning the betting of popular down-in-class greyhounds, is that it is almost impossible to get a decent price. Even quinielas involving down-graded dogs often pay less than $10.

Why are upgraded dogs so often overlooked in the wagering? To answer this, you must first understand the arithmetic of grading. Greyhounds are timed electronically in hundredths of a second, as compared with the archaic stopwatch timing of thoroughbreds in terms of a fifth of a second. What this means to the greyhound handicapper is that there is very little margin of error, and he had better have his arsenal of data strictly in order.

One body length of a greyhound crossing the finish line translates into seven-hundredths of a second. If he wins by 2½ lengths, the time of the place dog will be approximately 18-hundredths of a second slower than the winner's time. Times vary considerably at different tracks, due to soil conditions and the presence of moisture. However, at one specific meet, the times are amazingly consistent. At the Phoenix area tracks where my pups run, you can expect Grade A winners to run the 550-yard sprint course in approximately 30.90. A wet track would naturally raise winning times by as much as a half second.

It has been established, and here is the crux of my moving up in class advice, that roughly three lengths (.21) of a second separate the winners of each class. In other words, if 30.90 is a representative winning time for a Grade A race over a fast strip, then it follows that 31.11 would represent an average B win, 31.32 would be the norm for Grade C, while the less predictable Grade D times should level out around 31.53.

What does all this mean to us? A great deal, really, when you stop to consider that up-in-grade dogs are anathema to most handicappers. They dismiss them with nary a second glance, and then shake their heads in dismay and look for alibis when they come in at handsome odds. The key factor here is when an up-graded greyhound is an attractive commodity and when we should leave well enough alone.

Factors to consider are how convincingly our choice won his last outing and whether he is moving from unfavorable boxes to a favorable one this time. Naturally, if the performance times show that he most recently occupied the 1, 2 and 8 boxes, for instance, and he has now drawn the 6 hole, there is no valid reason to assume he will be a repeat winner in the higher grade. On the other hand, if the reverse is true and he will be breaking from an advantageous box, he will likely be a logical longshot pick, providing he meets the special requirement.

Remember, the three-length yardstick was used to measure the variance between average wins at the different grade levels. Reducing this differential to .21 of a second, we conclude that our potential selection must have won his last race by at least three lengths for us to give him a legitimate shot at the top spot this time around.

Unfortunately, most lower-grade races are won by less than a three-length margin, but when one is uncovered, it is a positive betting factor. The best place to find these "much the best" winners is often the pool of just recently-graduated maidens, young pups between the ages of 18 months and two years. They often come up with some lopsided wins in their march toward Grade A. If a greyhound is destined to be a legitimate A grade performer, he will generally shoot right up to the top with precious few stops along the way. If a racer has to struggle to finally attain Grade A status, the chances are he won't have the overall speed or savvy to stay there for long.

Class change is only one of eleven points I advocate in successfully handicapping a race, but it is undeniably one of the most important and easiest to spot for the beginner. Everyone jumps on the bandwagon for the downgraded dog. Why not be one of the fortunate few who recognizes the big payoff potential of the up-in-grade greyhound who won his last race convincingly and is moving into a starting box that is more to his liking?

Chapter 8

Jai Alai and the Magic Number 8

by Bill Keevers

Jai alai brings eight teams together in a round robin in every game. Each post position has its advantages and its handicaps. In horse racing, you don't always have the same number of pedigreed animals competing in every race. Sometimes it might be only four, at other times, a dozen. It all depends on weather the health of the horses or the whim of the trainer. You might pick something good out of the *Daily Racing Form* only to find your choice has been scratched.

At the track, post positions might be drawn, but at jai alai the matchmaker is going to place each team in the exact spot where it has an equal chance to win. Post positions are scientifically determined with much care and calculation.

Whether singles or doubles, there are always precisely eight teams in each game. And it's true that the low-numbered teams have an initial advantage. They play first, having the opportunity to score points before other teams come on the floor. When #1 and #2 come running out on the cancha, it's possible that the winner of that match could go right on with victories over #3, #4, #5, #6, #7, and #8. This makes a total score of seven points, or the game. This is "going all the way"—seven wins, no losses, But note that these are all single-point games and the team that makes this first round sweep has to win seven games.

It's true that any team can win all of its games but for logical reasons it isn't likely. First, opponents will be progressively harder to beat, a team that has racked up two, three or four wins, some of them exhausting contests, is going to be tired. The oncoming competitors are fresh. To go through a series of games without a rest is likely to be overtaxing.

Second, there's that law of averages, although Nick the Greek left us this legacy: "There is no law of averages, only the law of probabilities." But the physical factor is of importance; a rested team will beat a tired team most of the time.

The matchmaker assembles his playing card for each night 48 hours in advance. He is trying to equalize everything. He matches partners that can perform well together, and places them in the relative post positions where skills can give their opponents a head start, yet overcome the disadvantage.

In the early games, he will place the junior players. They are often teamed with a seasoned pro for balance. In the middle bracket, he will put the players who have proven themselves and are capable of taking any game. In the last two slots, and particularly #8, he will place the best players in that group.

Is this merely opinion? Not always. In the players' manager's office are big wide sheets on which are inscribed the record of every player on the roster. Each athlete is rated in many ways, but a control factor might be how many points he scores in each game. The statistics in the program will show how many games a player has won, but the matchmaker wants to know more than that. If a player is scoring three to four points in every game he plays, eventually he'll start to win games. Conversely, if he gets shut out too many times or scores a single point, he is not producing.

It isn't always a case of putting two high scorers together. Sometimes, two stars do not play well as a team. One might be trying to outdo his partner, forgetting that jai alai is largely a matter of good teamwork. It is also a fact that quite often two players of average ability play like whirlwinds when they are teamed together.

Physical condition is always a factor. A pelotari might have just recovered from an injury. He may be able to play, but not at his best, usually favoring a leg or an ankle. The matchmaker is also aware of "streaks." Jose or Arnaldo might be on a winning tear. Or one might be in a slump. These are all determining factors in matching the players, and putting the teams together.

In single games, it is even harder to figure equivalents. In the conventional double game, each player is on unfamiliar ground half the time. This is a fact his opponent is going to use to the best advantage. If he's a back court man, his adversary is going to try to keep him up front; but a front court man will be sent chasing way out in the back court alley. It's like asking a right fielder to play third base.

Look at your scorecard. If you really like the #8 combination, just remember the matchmaker put these fellows in the spot because he thought they were the best. This team can give up two or three points and overtake the leaders.

Team #8 has a handicap in reaching the floor last, but then another factor is in their favor. The #8 team only has to play one game for a single point. The early birds could collect only a solitary point by winning a game. On comes #8, and if this particular team is lucky enough or skillful enough to win, then every game thereafter is for two points. Number 8 can win a seven-point game with only four victories, unlike those patsies who went after all of those one-point games in the first round.

This is the feature in jai alai that makes it different from other sports. Racing horses or dogs run their one little stint and, win or lose, they are finished. Not so in jai alai. The pressure in this game doesn't really start until the second or third round. Sometimes there could even be a fourth round if they're all bunched.

Even if it drops its first game, #8 is still in the running, a wider handicap, of course, but the matchmaker didn't put this duo in the #8 slot without thinking it could overcome obstacles. Number 8 can come from behind, too. The only thing they have to beware of is an opposing team running out the score while they are blanketed in an advancing rotation position and not get another chance to play.

There is a psychological advantage in being #8. It's like batting in the clean-up #4 position in baseball. The other players know the matchmaker didn't pick these fellows' names out of a hat; he put them in #8 because he thought they could outplay the others, catch anybody who had a pointspread ahead of them. Experienced players also know that in a very long range compilation, #2 wins most games, #3 is next and #8 a very close third. This reverses the idea that getting the last chance in the round robin would put them out of the running.

A lot of people in Wall Street have gone broke playing the averages; poker players often do well with them. If you're a #8 enthusiast, take comfort in this fact: #8 may not win as often as, let's say #2 or #3, but it will pay more. Possibly because fewer people play #8, there's more in the pool when payoff time comes. In a tally of games at an eastern fronton these prices averaged out: Win—$14.80; Place—$8.60; Show—$6.30. If you're a quiniela player, the best 8 combination at the Hartford fronton in the season studied was 3 and 8. Next best was 1 and 8, with 4-8 and 5-8 as next in line. The full compilation is as follows:

Hartford Fronton: Quiniela with #8. 1981 Season

1-8 106 wins
2-8　55 wins
3-8 120 wins
4-8　90 wins
5-8　90 wins
6-8　58 wins
7-8　21 wins

The biggest winner was 2-3—with 181, but remember that a 2-3 quiniela usually pays in the $30 bracket. A 1-8 might pay $40-plus and other combinations progressively higher—up to the 7-8 which often pays over $100.

A lot of pelotarians play post positions exclusively. At Hartford in 1981, #8 did well in the post position category. In the game 3 classification, #8 finished first 34 times, just one win behind #3 which had 35. In game 4, #8 had 36 wins against #2's 38; in game 11, #8 chalked up 32 wins—against the leader #2's 35. Overall, #8 had a total of 344 wins compared to the top #2's 437. This is for wins only and does not include secondary finishes in the quinielas and perfectas.

In the perfecta classification, results at Hartford for the season were as follows:

#8 Perfecta: Combinations

Low Number First	High Number First
1-8 51 wins	8-1 53 wins
2-8 45 wins	8-2 40 wins
3-8 61 wins	8-3 59 wins
4-8 33 wins	8-4 57 wins
5-8 15 wins	8-5 58 wins
6-8 5 wins	8-6 53 wins
7-8 8 wins	8-7 13 wins

The leading perfecta combinations were 4 and 1 (101 wins) and 4 and 2 (95 wins).

For those who like to figure relationships between winning numbers in different contests, note that the 3 and 8 was the top quiniela combination. Numbers 3 and 8 were also the top winners in both sides of the perfecta.

Here are the leading three-numbered combinations in the

trifecta with 8 as a factor:

8-5-3-22 wins
3-8-4-20 wins
8-3-6-20 wins
8-6-3-20 wins

Note that all four of these winning numbers have an eight and a three. There must be a message there somewhere. Sticklers will also notice back in the perfecta compilation that the high number first won more often than the same number with the low number first. Putting the high number first won 333 times as compared to 218 wins for the low-first combo. This is traditional at other frontons also; on average, high first wins 60% of the time.

All of this might be needless advice to the seasoned perfecta player who almost invariably plays it both ways anyway. An extra $3 for the "other way" is usually good insurance. If you really like a number combination, play it both ways. That's the way horse bettors usually play the daily double. There is no sadder guy or gal in the fronton than someone holding a useless perfecta ticket played the "wrong way."

This chapter has dealt only with the jai alai fan who bets "the numbers." There are others who are dedicated "player" bettors. There is much logic to their choice. Who can deny that a good player will win more often than a player that has not reached his peak? Rod Carew will get more hits than a rookie. But in jai alai, the pelota can bounce eccentrically at times and even the best of players don't win all the time.

So even the fellow who only plays the best players—where is he likely to find them among the post positions? Theoretically, that little old matchmaker is going to put the best players in every set in the #8 spot. The #8s have to be capable of overcoming an early lead. Check the playing statistics in the program and see if that fellow in the #8 spot isn't well up in the averages. Study the payoffs and you'll notice that the #8s bring in more money than some of the other numbers.

A 1-2 quiniela usually pays around $30. The prominent 3-8 we have noticed here usually finds the ticket holder counting up to $50 at the cashier's window. Eights may not win quite as often as some numbers, but they do pay more on average.

It is important for bettors to know what the odds are on the game they're betting. Posted odds on the board will give you a pretty good idea, but in general your chances of selecting a winning ticket will improve if you will remember these incontrovertible odds: Any $2 quiniela combination will win once every 28 times. In the $3 perfecta the odds are 1 in 56. For a $6 trifecta box it's a 56 to 1 chance. The long shot $3 trifecta is 1 in 336. But you can get the high payoff: the box pays less, 1/3 of the posted trifecta price, as you are in effect betting only $1 on each combination.

Don't overlook the number eight. Discount the fact that this team doesn't come on the floor until last. Look at it this way—you are playing a well-rested team. Each jai alai game, believe it or not, develops a pattern as it progresses. Those very experienced #8s can sit there on the player's bench watching the whole game unfold. They can tell which players on the floor are on their game, which are showing off-form. If one team shoots out in front with two or three points, the #8s start to figure their strategy in how to beat them.

Every player on the roster has his own particular strong points and weaknesses. These fellows are real pros or the matchmaker wouldn't have given them the temporary handicap of placing them in the eighth spot. They know exactly where to place their shots so that the opposing front court or back court men will have difficulty in fielding them. Even in singles, where the strategy is keener, #8 will know what to do.

You can believe it—eight is a good solid number. In the wine fraternity in England there's a centuries-old saying: "Claret for boys, port for men; brandy for heroes." It takes a little more courage to play #8 at jai alai, but you'll get a hero's reward when you win. And you often will.

Jai Alai Terminology

BANKROLL—A set sum of money used to carry on business daily at frontons. Also used to describe money available to an individual for the sole purpose of gambling.

BREAKAGE—Monies in excess of actual payoffs for winning tickets. Prices calculated to nearest dime or nickle according to laws governing particular frontons.

CANCHA—Playing area of jai alai fronton.

CESTA—A combination glove and basket type object, strapped to the wrist of a jai alai player, used to catch and throw the ball (pelota) during a jai alai contest.

COMMISSION—Monies deducted from pari-mutuel pools to pay expenses and revenue necessary to a jai alai operation.

FAVORITE—Entry having more dollars bet on it than any other entry in the game.

FRONTS—Front wall of a cancha at jai alai frontons.

FRONTON—Name of building where jai alai is played.

HANDLE—Term used by frontons to designate volume of monies wagered.

JAI ALAI—A game of Basque origin used in some countries for pari-mutuel wagering in the same manner as horse or dog racing.

LATERAL—Name used for the side wall of the cancha at a jai alai fronton.

MOONLIGHTERS—Fronton employees having steady employment in other fields and using fronton earnings as a supplement to their regular income.

ODDS—Number indicating amount of profit per dollar to be paid to holders of winning pari-mutuel tickets.

PARI-MUTUELS—A system of betting, whereby the holders of winning tickets are paid in proportion to the sums they have wagered.

PARTIDO SYSTEM—Jai alai games played by two individuals or two sets of partners only. The winner is decided when one player or one team has reached a pre-designated number of points (usually 25 to 35 points). It is not possible to use the pari-mutuel system for partido games except for win pools.

PAST PERFORMANCE—Documented records of previous efforts of jai alai players.

PER CAPITA—Average amount bet by each customer during a day's business at a fronton.

PURSE—Prize money earned by winning jai alai players.

RACING COMMISSION—An appointed body of men and women which governs and polices jai alai in states where legislation has been passed to permit use of the pari-mutuel system in connection with this sport. Usually appointed by the governor of the state.

REBOTE—Back wall of a cancha at a jai alai fronton.

SCRATCH—An entry listed to compete in a game, but withdrawn after becoming an official entry, due to illness, injury, or other bona fide reasons.

STEWARDS—Racing officials charged with the duty of making sure jai alai games are carried out in conformance with rules set down by the Racing Commission in the state where these contests are being held.

STOOPERS—Name given to persons looking for valid tickets discarded mistakenly by patrons at a fronton. This practice is prohibited by law in most states.

TIP SHEETS—Selections of professional handicappers for sale to patrons desiring help in deciding which entry to wager on.

TOUTS—Persons furnishing their selections to patrons in return for a portion of the amount of money collected, should their selections win. Practice discouraged at all frontons and illegal at most.

Section Three
HORSE RACING

Beating the horses requires, first of all, an understanding of the basics of reading the *Racing Form* and secondly attention to the finer points of the game. This section provides knowledge of both the basics and some of the subtleties.

Section Three
HORSE RACING

Chapter 9

Thoroughbred Racing's Best Bet

by Earl Sklar

This chapter will furnish you with what I feel is the best system bet in racing, perhaps the best wager available in any form of gambling. It involves a situation which is easily detectable by the most novice racing fan. This play takes different forms, but the one with which we will concern ourselves wins approximately 66% of the time and has an average payoff of 3 or 4 to 1. Other forms of this bet can produce much higher prices, but let's get comfortable with the basic system first.

When it comes to handicapping, the winning horseplayer must learn to trust and automatically bet certain situations which we can call our "system plays." When the right circumstances occur, they become an automatic play no matter what other horses are in the race. (If there are two or more horses that fit the same system, pass up the race for now.)

This particular bet will occur in maiden races; the races that most people find so difficult really turn out to be very simple—and most profitable. *When a horse runs at least one good race in a straight maiden race, it is almost a certain winner when dropped in class into a lower-level maiden claiming race.*

Let's examine the difference between straight maidens and maiden claiming races, as well as the structures of these races. The straight maiden race is the highest class maiden race. Horses that run in these races cannot be claimed. If a horse is not good enough to compete in a straight maiden race, it then runs in the maiden claiming races. Here, they are eligible to be purchased by anyone who is willing to put up the claiming price of the individual race.

I am a handicapper of the Southern California tracks (Hollywood Park, Santa Anita, and Del Mar). At these tracks, the maiden claiming races begin with a claiming price of $20,000; then up to $25,000, $32,000, $40,000 and finally $50,000. The straight maiden race is above all these in racing class.

Any horse that has run at least one good race in a straight maiden race and is today being dropped in class into a maiden claimer will be called a "dropper"; maiden claiming races will be called "claimers."

If our dropper is being raced today in a $50,000 claimer, it is not a play. This is because there are just too many good horses in a $50,000 race. In addition, there will probably be other droppers. We would therefore begin at the $40,000 level.

Of course, the $32,000 level is easier yet, and at $25,000 and $20,000 it's like stealing! *Droppers running at these lower levels usually win by many open lengths!*

Before we get into examples of droppers, I'd like to briefly mention maidens coming from different tracks. In my opinion, Southern California and New York (Aqueduct, Belmont, and Saratoga) racing are a cut above the rest of the nation.

It is not my intention to offend anyone in Florida, Chicago, or any of the other fine tracks throughout the country; they all have fine racing programs. However, one reason racing in California and New York has a slightly better class of horses is the size of the purses. The most money draws the best horses. Also, take a look at the top jockeys and you'll find the majority located on these two racing circuits.

Therefore, when I'm playing horses in Southern California, a dropper is only a bet when being dropped from New York or Southern California straight maidens. Wherever you are playing horses, a dropper is only an automatic bet when coming from a comparable or better class track.

Table 9-1 contains the past performances of horses which are excellent examples of the maiden dropper system described in this chapter.

These horses have repeatedly run good races to straights, all winning in the $40,000 level of maiden claiming and paying prices from 8-5 to 4-1.

Table 9-1

Flint Image — Ch. g. 4, by Gunflint—Edee's Image, by Cornish Prince
Br.—Kinship Syndicate (Fla) — 1981 5 1 0 1 $11,125
Own.—Summa Stable & Gordy — 119 — Tr.—Wheeler Robert L — $25,000 — 1980 1 M 0 0

23May81-4Hol	6f	:221 :452 1:103ft	4	123	1hd	12½	12	11¼	Pierce D10	M40000	84	FlintImage,HawiinSnd,HppyEnvoy	11
4Mar81-4SA	6f	:213 :443 1:10 ft	9	118	14½	12½	1½	55½	Pierce D1	Mdn	83	Sky Yarder, L'Oiseleur, Bangalero	8
18Feb81-6SA	6f	:214 :444 1:10 ft	2½	117	11	2½	43¾	811	Pincay L Jr9	Mdn	78	TonysLnding,L'Oiseleur,FreeRelity	10
4Feb81-6SA	6½f	:214 :443 1:164ft	8	117	21	2hd	2½	32¾	Pincay L Jr3	Mdn	83	Territorial,MulliganStew,FlintImge	7
22Jan81-6SA	6½f	:212 :44 1:161ft	11	117	2hd	21	43½	511	Pincay L Jr6	Mdn	78	Resistance, PacificMorn,Territorial	9
27Dec80-6SA	6f	:212 :434 1:091ft	6½	119	76¼	912	1117	1122	Shoemaker W9	Mdn	71	HyDickrn,TonysLnding,BtlnPockt	12

Jun 2 Hol 5f ft 1:002 h — May 22 Hol 3f ft :35 h — ●May 16 Hol 3f ft :351 h — May 9 Hol 3f ft :352 h

Ack Ack Attack — Dk. b. or br. h. 5, by Ack Ack—Sheila Jan, by Nigromante
Br.—Jocoy & Whittingham (Ky) — 1980 9 1 2 2 $21,675
Own.—Jocoy & Whittingham — 114 — Tr.—Whittingham Charles — Turf 2 0 1 1 $7,700

29Jun80-7Hol	1⅛	Ⓣ:472 1:114 1:482fm	6	1095	57½	55	62¼	23	McGurn C5	Alw	85	Guarntee,AckAckAttck,SummitRun	9
13Jun80-7Hol	1	Ⓣ:462 1:11 1:36 fm	32	1095	811	97½	75	3hd	McGurn C9	Alw	89	CardGame,CaraalSol,AckAckAttck	10
1Jun80-3Hol	1	:452 1:111 1:372ft	*8-5	1175	410	11	1½	13½	McGurn C8	M40000	79	AckAckAttck,ElTiburon,ReglMesur	9
5Apr80-4SA	1	:462 1:11 1:361ft	3¼	118	54	3nk	33	43¾	Pincay L Jr7	Mdn	84	Finisterre, Capital C.,ChiefGummo	10
28Mar80-6SA	1 1/16	:461 1:114 1:443ft	9-5	118	4¾	2hd	1½	3¾	Shoemaker W8	Mdn	77	Grmntes,ChifGummo,AckAckAttck	8
14Mar80-6SA	1 1/16	:46 1:11 1:432ft	4½	118	21	3½	22½	28	Shoemaker W8	Mdn	76	AugustIc,AckAckAttck,SuprScott	12
27Feb80-4SA	6f	:221 :452 1:094ft	5½	117	52	74¼	77¾	512	Shoemaker W10	Mdn	78	Barnt, Chieftains Prince,CapitalC.	12
30Jan80-6SA	6f	:22 :454 1:121gd	3½	117	54	65½	68¾	66¼	Shoemaker W6	Mdn	72	Minnemac, El Romeo, For Real	12
1Jan80-6SA	6f	:214 :443 1:092ft	3	117	73¾	911	813	512	Shoemaker W11	Mdn	80	Black Hood, Vaslov, Chicago	12

May 13 Hol 5f ft 1:001 h — May 8 Hol 1 ft 1:411 h — May 3 Hol 1 ft 1:412 h — Apr 28 Hol 7f ft 1:281 h

Granja Muchacha — Ch. f. 4, by Envoy—Bayful, by Our Babu
Br.—Granja Vista del Rio (Cal) — 1981 6 1 0 0 $11,000
Own.—Granja Vista del Rio Stable — 113 — Tr.—Palma Hector O — 1980 0 M 0 0

29Dec81-4SA	6f	:221 :452 1:111ft	3½e	117	11	13	13	14¼	Sibille R7	ⒻM40000	82	GranjMuchch,Tesble,NuticlPower	10
14Nov81-6Hol	6f	:22 :452 1:104ft	4¾e	119	3nk	53¾	79½	914	Hawley S1	ⒻMdn	69	Cy Fi, Palisair, Jujube	12
21Mar81-3SA	6f	:222 :461 1:12 gd	4¾	117	1½	2½	31½	45¾	Pierce D6	ⒻⓈMdn	73	Doon'sLady,SucyBit,LovelyRomnce	8
21Feb81-3SA	6f	:214 :444 1:092ft	6½	117	1hd	2hd	34½	413	Hawley S2	ⒻⓈMdn	79	GlttrHttr,Mrlyn'sDlght,LovlyRomnc	9
8Feb81-3SA	6f	:212 :44 1:091ft	9	117	31	3nk	31	52¾	Hawley S4	ⒻMdn	90	BrightLdy,WingingIt,Mrilyn'sDlight	6
24Jan81-3SA	6½f	:213 :444 1:164ft	5½	117	42½	3½	45½	46¾	Hawley S5	ⒻⓈMdn	79	IntrviwTim,BrightLdy,BluTmptton	10

Jan 14 SA 4f ft :474 h — Dec 24 Hol tr.t 5f ft 1:05 h — Dec 18 Hol 3f ft :361 h — Dec 12 Hol 5f ft 1:01 h

Copyright © 1982, by Daily Racing Form, Inc. Reprinted with permission of copyright owner.

Belltrista in Table 9-2 showed very good form in her first race on September 11, but ran into a group of maidens that were a little too fast for her on September 18. This happens often as the quality of maidens vary. So, if our dropper does poorly in fast straight races, this will usually lead to a better price in the claimer. The public reacts very negatively to a horse with a poor last race. When dropped into a $32,000 race, *Belltrista* ran to an easy win at 8 to 1.

Table 9-2

Belltrista 113
Own.—D'Onofrio-Hoover-Wlmsn
B. f. 2, by Mr Cockatoo—Flashy Dish, by Petrone
Br.—Hoover & Williamson (Cal)
Tr.—Mazzone Paul A
1981 3 1 0 1 $9,500

```
14Oct81-3SA  6f  .221 .454 1:113ft  8  115  1hd 22 13 13½  McHrguDG5  ⑥M32000 80  Belltrista,TripleMach,AegenQueen 12
18Sep81-4Omf 6f  .222 .454 1:109ft  6½ 117  41½ 69 6¹¹ 7¹⁴  Ortega L E5  ⑦Mdn 71  Bit of Beau, Avigaition,DoubleTuff 8
11Sep81-7Omf 6f  .222 .463 1:112ft  22 1125 3¹ 3½ 32 34  SchnvldtCP4  ⑦Mdn 77  StudentbodyRight,JsminJul,Bltrnst 6
Nov 3 SA tr.1 4ft .49³h    Oct 29 SA 4f ft .51h    Oct 11 SA 4f ft :49h    Oct 6 SA 4f ft :49¹h
```

Hualalai 119
Own.—Paniolo Ranch
Ch. f. 3, by Gallant Romeo—Don't Get Caught, by Watch Your Step
Br.—Wooden Horse Investments (Ky)
Tr.—Clyne Vincent
1981 5 1 1 0 $13,050
1980 2 M 0 0 $325

```
17Apr81-6SA   6f   .214 .45  1:11 ft   8   117  11½ 12 13 11  GonzlzA,Jr10  ⑥M40000 84  Hualalai,GranjaDuquesa,AGiftAgin 12
12Apr81-3SA   6f   .214 .45  1:093ft   20  117  1hd 22 25 21⁴  Gonzalez A Jr7  ⑦Mdn 77  Ms. Hapa Haole,Hualalai,BlueBaba 11
15Mar81-3SA   6½f  .22  .45² 1:171ft   42  1125 3nk 32 55⅜ 81³  Tejada V M,Jr3  ⑦Mdn 71  Floppy Miss,Deceptive,FoolishGirl 12
28Feb81-4SA   6½f  .213 .45¹ 1:174sy   2½e 117  14 11 39 1228  VldiviesoHA12  ⑦Mdn 53  Aspermont,Aggrndizement,Dcptiv 12
22Feb81-3SA   6f   .212 .442 1:102ft   93  117  43½ 56⅜ 78⅜ 56  ValdiviesOHA9  ⑦Mdn 81  Bankable,CanYouDigIt,ZealousCat 11
18Oct80-4SA   6f   .214 .443 1:101ft   68  115  2¹½ 25 36 5¹¹  Gonzalez A Jr5  ⑦Mdn 77  Track Jester, Done Wrong,Lu'x'gal 11
17Sep80-11Dmf 6f   .212 .444 1:102ft   22  114  8⁷⅜ 9¹⁴ 9¹⁷ 820  GiAJr1  ⑦Cardiff Sea 66  IrishArrivl,ForStekeping,Enggingly 9
Apr 11 SA 3f ft .36³h
```

Copyright © 1982, by Daily Racing Form Inc. Reprinted with permission of copyright owner.

Hualalai in Table 9-2 showed partial form in her early races, then ran second on April 12 in an exceptionally fast race (109 3/5 final time). In this race, she ran head to head with the winner, who drew off to win by many lengths, yet *Hualalai* still beat nine other straight maidens. When dropped into a claimer, after coming out of such a fast race, she was an easy winner at 8 to 1.

This chapter presents a system play that produces relatively low-priced horses. I have discovered through record keeping that this system can produce a huge profit.

The winning horseplayer must be able to spot and bet higher-priced horses. Price horses begin at 5 to 1, with 10 to 1 and up being where the real profits are. Only by knowing and understanding everything that is going on at your track can you uncover horses with a real chance at a price.

Chapter 10

Betting a Horse of a Different Color

by Frank Cotolo

The racing enthusiast headed for the British Isles in search of action had bloody well better do some homework first. Take it from me, mate, they have a way of playing horses that is as different from the American system as is the money you lay down. I learned the hard way, losing a few quid here and there by giving in to the gambler's impulse to have some action. But I became bent on assimilating their modus operandi to ensure my selections. And once I did, I collected with assurance instead of relief. It really isn't that difficult if you take the time to observe, and it certainly is more profitable.

First, concentrate only on flat racing. Forget about the greyhounds—the flats are far more consistent and reliable. The factors you can use to handicap horses there will serve your pounds far better than those factors available for thoroughbred dogs. And the action on tap for flat betting is plentiful. Three tracks can be holding meets concurrently and will all be playable via betting parlors. Off-track bookmakers are abundant throughout the country. Clean and comfortable organizations like William Hill, Mecca, and Playboy Bookmakers provide the public with all the data needed to make an educated wager. In fact, there is more info clinging to the walls of these parlors than you will ever find at an English track.

This brings us to the second, and a most important, tip: Don't go to a racetrack to bet. What I mean is if you are into making a few pounds, the bookmakers at the parlors are far more easy to deal with than the characters on the scene. At the racetrack itself there is a distracting chaos going on with the bookies.

You see, very few people are playing what the British call the *Tote*, which is the closest thing to pari-mutuel wagering they have. It stands to reason, too. Placing a bet with the Tote means relying on morning odds. The track does not have a tote board, so there is no visible record as to how odds change with the betting. The pool is simply divided after the race into however many people have wagered on that entry. The bookies, on the other hand, change their odds constantly up to post time and in some cases you can catch a horse who winds up at 5-2 by holding a bookie ticket giving you 6-1 on that same horse.

This is because a bookie pays whatever odds you bet at, regardless of later changes. If you bet a horse at 10-1 and he wins, you will be paid 10-1 even if that particular bookie dropped the odds to 6-5 before post. It sure sounds great, eh? But it takes insurmountable concentration to keep up with these blokes. You see, there are a lot of them around, shouting like carnival hawks while scores of gamblers dart from one to another in search of bargains. It is a certified circus of confusion unless you have spent years getting into the flow.

When I was at Ripon Racecourse one evening, I was pushed and shoved relentlessly by patrons trying to reach a bookie who was giving 6-1 on a horse that another had just dropped to 3-1. One has to be quick, you understand, for each bookie has patrolling the grounds what is known as a *Tic-Tac Man*. Working along with his respective bookie, the Tic-Tac Man spies on the other bookies and signals over to his partner with flamboyant gesticulations, indicating to him that odds have dropped on a particular horse. The bookie, seeing the sign from the Tic-Tacker, quickly goes to the sponge and erases the odds on his little blackboard, reducing them to whatever the Tic-Tacker has signaled.

It is not unusual to see a gambler cover the higher chalked odds, if his hand is quick enough, before the bookie sponges them, ensuring the bet at the pre-Tic-Tacked price. These are gamblers who have a million eyes, no doubt from training themselves to catch the Tic-Tacker as the hand signals are thrown. Only a seasoned patron would be able to cash in on this action. As for myself, I wound up getting a 4-5 ticket that a veteran would be paid 7-1 on. Remember, you're on their turf, so you cannot expect to be as sharp as they are.

The Tote, on the other hand, is extremely calm, and now you know why—the payoffs are terrible. Most of the people playing the Tote are those attendees who are at the track for the social aspect. Indeed, there is a large number of these, undaunted by the likes of odds, hanging around to spin gossip with neighbors and business mates. You can spot them easily: They're regally dressed, proper in their speech and they have a stuffy demureness about them.

They play the Tote because the betting is secondary to the diatribes. And they'll spend far more money on drinks than they ever will backing a horse. The sport is the backdrop to a social occasion, a night out away from the telly. In short, they are anything but gamblers.

So go to the racetrack like you would visit Big Ben. It is a wonderful tourist trip. The tracks are as old and quaint as the patrons' accents, and beautifully manicured and untouched by progress. Most of them repose in a time warp, especially the tracks in the Yorkshires. Courses like Thirsk and Ponterfract are landmarks of structural tradition.

Progress has no clout within the confines of these courses. There are no television monitors, the grandstands are concrete slats, the turf is manually pounded between races. It is culturally engrossing. But it is not the place to gamble seriously on anything except a good roll of film.

Now, at the betting parlors you may find more veteran gamblers, but because the bookie is a progressive machine, you will not be burdened with diversions. For one, the parlor is taking book on as many cards as are being held that day, regardless of where in the Kingdom they originate. For example, you may be able to bet on the events at Edinburgh in Scotland while keeping tabs on the action at Folkestone on the southeast shore.

When such activity is happening, you'll notice the times of the races in concurrent running tracks are scheduled so as not to conflict with betting. For instance, the Edinburgh card will run its events at 2:15, 2:45, 3:15, etc., while the Folkestone races will be at 2:30, 3:00, and 3:30. This gives the parlor bettor a chance to have action in all 12 races (note that there are rarely more than six races per card).

Should three tracks be going, there might be less time between the events on each card, but the races will never be at the same time. Thus, you could bet as many as 18 races in a four-hour period. That's action!

What some might consider a major setback is the fact that no detailed past performance info (as we would be accustomed to) is available. The closest things to it are papers like *The Sporting News* and *Sporting Chronicle*. Seasoned handicappers publish their opinions on entries based on past performances, jockey capability and, of course, the track.

It is the very nature of British meets not to be at one track for more than four days at a time, so a horse has little chance of accumulating a track form. Oddly enough, these animals seem to make the transitions with an adaptation superior to that of American-breds. Again, they are used to their variables, so don't go betting horses for courses, so to speak.

You can trust a handicapper if he touts a nag to a certain course contour (and there are many different ovals to study, some undulating and others with steep hills in the stretch). Just forget about where you are and key in on how the horse performed in his last few outings. I must say, I almost went blind getting used to reading these publications. The type is microscopic and the abbreviations for key information have got to be studied in order to scout a winner. All you need is concentration, and you'll be in a more suitable atmosphere for that at a parlor.

I found, after an empirical study of a hundred or so races, that form holds up pretty well with these critters, despite the condition of the track or the variation of the course. I saw horses who won in the mud at Bath (which has an uphill finish) take a two-week rest and return to go at Goodwood (where there are sharp turns) on firm ground at a different distance, and stand up. These animals are trained for a certain strength within their system and it seems you can trust them to perform with consistency regardless of what might appear to be a crucial variable.

I suggest you take little heed of the course and conditions of that day and focus on two things: the horse in its last run and the jockey. The jockey is a factor you cannot overlook. Learn to recognize these names; I doubt if many will be familiar to you. Aside from famous expatriate Steve Cauthen, the remainders should be fresh. But you should be aware that fellows like Greville Starkey, Lester Piggot, Eddie Hide and Pat Eddery can get the most out of a promising entry. Always give "points" to their mounts, even when they look particularly dim in their chances.

Foremost, though, will be the animal itself. If it has been with the finishers of late, or in some photos, depend on a similar performance. I found that you can. Rarely does a horse have a lucky second finish and trail the field next time out. I say rarely because, as in any horse racing, we are dealing with only so many known facts. All in all, from my experience, I was more than surprised to see horses in shape stay in shape with the facts I did find.

Class is another matter. There are no claiming events or conditioned races as we know it. Races are all named; the British are big on the names as opposed to the numbers. It would appear these events are all stakes races of a sort, because they are. There are handicaps, stakes, championships and cups. All races do have conditions, and these conditions should be given an eye. Know whether you're dealing with maidens or older stock, but don't harp on it. Form is more important than class dropping or stepping up.

I cannot figure out why, but to my estimation there is too much weight put into these factors in British horse racing. When I noticed a fast horse, I bet on him being fast coming off a maiden event into a stakes and was proven right with a winning slip. The right jockey on the horse who runs will add to the possibility of a good showing. For some unknown reason, these animals seem to fall into the all-things-being-equal syndrome once they leave the gate.

This is not to say there aren't some who stand out or some who can be ruled out for many reasons; it is to point out that class just doesn't have the clout as consistently as it does in American venture. Perhaps this is a reason why all American horses are worth a look when they are entered in Great Britain events, and vice versa. That is another thing to look for: horses asterisked U.S.A. are always a danger over there, especially with a decent rider. The horses adapt quicker than their stateside bettors, I dare declare!

Now you have a basic handle on the variables and you've chosen a bet. You are basing your selection on form first, jockey second, and leaving the rest to luck. So now's the time to go into your pocket and put your money where your facts are. Because you are at a parlor, you will be privy to seeing odds change as they are bet at the track. Computer television screens compile the information and flash it regularly. As I have mentioned, you are getting more input as to public choices at the parlor since no tote boards are flashing at the tracks. In reasonable comfort at the parlor, you are watching each entry being backed. Of course, if you win you will get closing odds, but being American you are used to that anyway.

A word or two now on the showing of these odds. You will find some foreign to you, like 2-7, 30-100, 4-9, 8-15. They are what I began to call in-between odds, in that there were levels of rising and dropping between the ones we would be used to. Accompanying this chapter is Table 10-1 with all the levels that could flash from 2-7 to 9-1:

Table 10–1

Odds Chart	
2-7	13-8
30-100	7-4
1-3	15-8
4-11	2-1
2-5	9-4
4-9	5-2
1-2	11-4
8-15	3-1
4-7	100-30
8-13	7-2
4-6	4-1
8-11	9-2
4-5	5-1
5-6	11-2
10-11	6-1
Evens	13-2
11-10	7-1
6-5	15-2
5-4	8-1
11-8	17-2
6-4	9-1

Now you've got an idea of what your selection should go off at, but what is the denomination of "one"? Here's where the British really make it easy. The minimum wager at a parlor is 20 pence (the equivalent of approximately 37 cents). Some bookies will take 5-pence bets but, regardless of the minimum, the 'one' in your odds is based on the 10-pence denomination. Thus, betting 10 pence on an 11-4 closing horse would return 37½ pence; 50 pence on the same horse would return one pound, 87½ pence; and a one-pound wager on the 11-4 shot gives you 3 pounds, 75 pence.

This is all before taxes. To reduce any eating away of winning profits because of tax, the bettor can pay the appropriate percentage when he first wagers. Scales telling what amount of tax to pay are posted throughout the parlor. It is a smart idea to pay whatever extra tax there is in the beginning because statistics, for reasons we will not delve into, indicate a savings in the long run.

British racing events start with many more entries than ours. As many as 40 horses can be listed before declarations and scratches, but horses retain their original post numbers. It is not uncommon to see the #15 horse win from post position #1. Yet, this is not really important.

First of all, post position is just not that important to the handicapper. At whatever course there is racing, the appropriate papers will usually specify if there is an advantage to the high or low draw. But even then you'll notice that it usually reads "slight advantage."

Second, you will not be betting numbers. I mentioned the British were big on names and here's where it is proven to the utmost. Anytime you are betting a horse, you must know the horse's name—that is how you will ensure your bet when you lay down your money.

The parlor supplies slips with carbons attached. You write in the name of the horse you are betting, the track and race time (remember, races are distinguished by the time of post, not by their position on the card. There's no fifth at Ripon or third at Sandown; there's only the 2:15, the 3:45, or the 4:10). So you indicate your win selection by name with the track time number and the amount you bet (adding tax if you're smart) and hold the receipt.

All along, I hope you've realized, I've been discussing betting to win. It is not the only way you can bet, but place and show wagering is, in a sense, foreign to Britons. You can, though, play their version of an exacta (or perfecta as the case may be). This is called a *forecast* and you can play it in any race unless otherwise indicated. As with an exacta, the first and second selections must arrive at the wire in that order. You can (and always should) reverse the two. Don't get shut down because you didn't lay out an extra few pence.

The forecast is a good deal, especially if you are dealing with a real favorite, like a 30-100 shot, and there's another entity you would like to back. With favorites winning as much as they do, a forecast can reap decent winnings—more than the wad you could place on a 30-100 shot, which on one pound would return only 29 pence profit. That same one pound on a winning forecast with the 30-100 shot on top and, say, a 14-1 placing gives you the forecast payoff (which could be upward of 50 pence to the ten).

On a pound, you have bought the forecast 10 times. Should it pay 50 pence, you have 5 pounds coming to you—a better profit than the win bet. Reverse it, I say, for if the photo should put that 14-1 a hair up on the big favorite, you're really into some profits.

At the parlor, you will be able to hear the call of every race. They are piped in over the sound system as the race is being run. And as soon as the result is official, you can collect. Moments later another race will be going off, especially if there are three cards that day, so you should get accustomed to the rapidity of this pace. With so much action, you can set your own pace, canceling out events that you simply do not feel for.

Give yourself some breathing room. I found that a two-race layoff for a cup of tea at a nearby pub did wonders for my return; it is simply madness to attempt to play every event. As a gambler, you know as well as I some races are just not worth the effort or investment. So cut them off your itinerary, take a ten break and get some air. (These parlors can get smoky—the British puff away intensely.) Clear your head; it never hurts your decision-making capabilities.

No stone is really left unturned when it comes to the types of betting. There are scores of schemes available, glossaries of which are available at the parlors should you wish to get into some exotic wagering. There are Accumulators, Doubles, Trebels, Dundee Shuffles, Flags, Fidos, Goliaths, Harlequins, Double Laps, Rounders, Roundabouts, Polys, Union Jacks, Trixies, Yankees and many more. My suggestion is to stick to finding the winners and at the most invest in some forecasts. These special schemes get mighty involved and the more you study the schemes, the less time you have to handicap.

In my travels from north to south, I played a remarkable amount of races. In toto, I came out ahead, simply by concentrating on the factors I have discussed in this chapter. There's always more to learn and a million ways of doing it better, but that's up to you. How intensely you get involved in handicapping is a personal matter. Just remember that if you are returning to the U.S.A. you are going to leave the British to their ways. I hope that this will help you make an easy transition for your stay, so you can have yourself a bloody good time—win, lose or draw.

The Tracks

English race courses are graded in groups according to levels of prize money and horse quality. A horse may drop in class simply by changing courses. The classifications are:

Flat

Group 1: Ascot, Ayr, Doncaster, Epsom, Goodwood, Haydock, Kempton, Newbury, Newcastle, Sandown, York.

Group 2: Brighton, Chester, Lingfield, Redcar, Ripon, Salisbury, Thirsk.

Group 3: Bath, Beverley, Chepstow, Hamilton, Leicester, Nottingham, Pontefract, Windsor, Yarmouth.

Group 4: Catterick, Carlisle, Edinburgh, Folkestone, Warwick, Wolverhampton.

Jumping

Group 1: Ascot, Ayr, Cheltenham, Doncaster, Haydock, Kempton, Liverpool, Newbury, Newcastle, Sandown.

Group 2: Chepstow, Fontwell, Lingfield, Newton Abbot, Wetherby.

Group 3: Catterick, Folkestone, Huntington, Leicester, Market Rasen, Nottingham, Plumpton, Stratford, Uttoxeter, Warwick, Wincanton, Windsor, Wolverhampton, Worcester.

Group 4: Bangor-on-Dee, Carlisle, Cartmel, Devon and Exeter, Fakenham, Hereford, Hexham, Kelso, Ludlow, Perth, Sedgefield, Southwell, Taunton, Towcester.

Chapter 11

The Basics of the Racing Form

by Eric Stoff

Why read the *Racing Form?* Well, it's based on the same premise as the rest of the information in this book: When it comes to betting the thoroughbreds you can either make the selections yourself, based on the information provided by the *Racing Form,* or you can depend on blind luck or someone else's picks.

The *Racing Form* is the trade name for the past performances or racing history of all of the horses running in today's races. The ten lines on the chart represent the last ten races each horse has run. When handicapping, you are required to read the charts and compare the information to the chart of the next horse. In this way, you can determine which animal has the advantage or the ability to win today's race. Of course, the difficulty arises in the relative importance given to each of the many pieces of information, but let's outline some clear examples (refer to Table 11-1).

Date—If today's race is in April of 1983 and the horse last ran in June of '82, a question of condition arises. Physically sound thoroughbreds generally run at least once a month, with most running every two weeks. As in all of the following explanations, there are frequent exceptions to these guidelines.

Racetrack—A horse which ran its last race at a small track in

Table 11-1

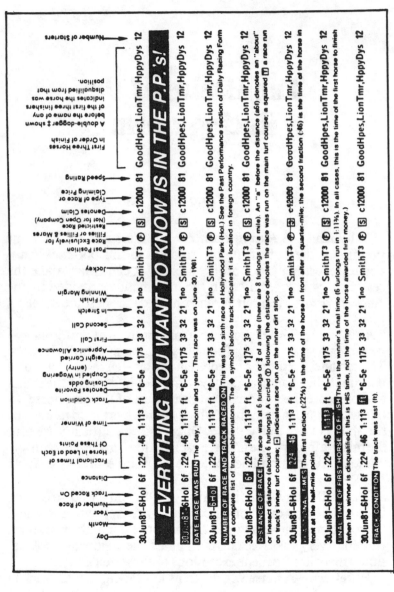

EVERYTHING YOU WANT TO KNOW IS IN THE P.P.'s!

Number of Starters	
First Three Horses In Order of Finish — A double-dagger ‡ shown before the name of any of the first three finishers indicates the horse was disqualified from that position.	
Speed Rating	
Type of Race or Claiming Price	
Denotes Claim (Not for Open Company)	
Restricted Race	
Race Exclusively for Fillies or Fillies & Mares	
Post Position	
Jockey	
Winning Margin	
At Finish	
In Stretch	
Second Call	
First Call	
Apprentice Allowance	
Weight Carried	
Coupled in Wagering (entry)	
Closing odds	
Denotes Favorite	
Track Condition	
Time of Winner	
Fractional Times of Horse in Lead at Each Of These Points	
Distance	
Track Raced On	
Number of Race	
Year	
Month	
Day	

30Jun81-6Hol 6f :224 :46 1:113 ft *6-5e 1175 33 32 21 1no SmithT3 ⓣ Ⓢ c12000 81 GoodHpes,LionTmr,HppyDys 12

DATE RACE WAS RUN The day, month and year. This race was on June 30, 1981.

NUMBER OF RACE AND TRACK RACED ON This was the sixth race at Hollywood Park (Hol.) See the Past Performance section of Daily Racing Form for a complete list of track abbreviations. The ◆ symbol before track indicates it is located in foreign country.

30Jun81-6Hol 6f :224 :46 1:113 ft *6-5e 1175 33 32 21 1no SmithT3 ⓣ Ⓢ c12000 81 GoodHpes,LionTmr,HppyDys 12

DISTANCE OF RACE The race was at 6 furlongs or ¾ of a mile (there are 8 furlongs in a mile). An "a" before the distance (a6f) denotes an "about" or inexact distance (about 6 furlongs). A circled Ⓣ following the distance denotes the race was run on the main turf course; a squared T a race run on track's inner turf course; ⊡ indicates race run on the inner dirt strip.

30Jun81-6Hol 6f :224 :46 1:113 ft *6-5e 1175 33 32 21 1no SmithT3 ⓣ Ⓢ c12000 81 GoodHpes,LionTmr,HppyDys 12

FRACTIONAL TIMES The first fraction (:22¾). The second fraction (:22½) is the time of the horse in front after a quarter-mile; the second fraction (:46) is the time of the horse in front at the half-mile point.

30Jun81-6Hol 6f :224 :46 1:113 ft *6-5e 1175 33 32 21 1no SmithT3 ⓣ Ⓢ c12000 81 GoodHpes,LionTmr,HppyDys 12

FINAL TIME OF FIRST HORSE TO FINISH This is the winner's final time (6 furlongs run in 1:11¾). In all cases, this is the time of the first horse to finish (when the winner is disqualified, thus is HIS time, not the time of the horse awarded first money.)

30Jun81-6Hol 6f :224 :46 1:113 ft *6-5e 1175 33 32 21 1no SmithT3 ⓣ Ⓢ c12000 81 GoodHpes,LionTmr,HppyDys 12

TRACK CONDITION The track was fast (ft).

Table 11-1 (continued)

30Jun81-6Hol 6f :224 :46 1:113 ft **6:5:5e** 1175 33 32 21 1no SmithT3 Ⓕ Ⓢ c12000 81 GoodHpes,LionTmr,HppyDys 12

APPROXIMATE CLOSING ODDS The horse was approximately 6.5 in the wagering. An asterisk (*) preceding the odds indicates the horse was the favorite; an "e" following the odds that it was part of an entry (two or more horses coupled in the wagering); an "f" that horse was in the mutuel field.

30Jun81-6Hol 6f :224 :46 1:113 ft *6-5e **1175** 33 32 21 1no SmithT3 Ⓕ Ⓢ c12000 81 GoodHpes,LionTmr,HppyDys 12

WEIGHT CARRIED IN THIS RACE The horse carried 117 pounds. The superior (small) figure following the weight indicates that, in this instance, a 5-pound apprentice allowance was claimed. When an apprentice allowance is claimed, the exact amount of the claim is listed.

30Jun81-6Hol 6f :224 :46 1:113 ft *6-5e 1175 **33** 32 21 1no SmithT3 Ⓕ Ⓢ c12000 81 GoodHpes,LionTmr,HppyDys 12

FIRST CALL The horse was running third, three lengths behind the leader at this stage of the race (at the ¼ mile in this instance). The larger figure indicates the horse's running position, the superior figure his total margin behind the leader. If he had been in front at this point (1³), the superior figure would indicated the margin by which he had been leading the second horse

30Jun81-6Hol 6f :224 :46 1:113 ft *6-5e 1175 33 **32** 21 1no SmithT3 Ⓕ Ⓢ c12000 81 GoodHpes,LionTmr,HppyDys 12

SECOND CALL The horse was third at this stage of the race (at the ½ mile in this instance), two lengths behind the leader.

30Jun81-6Hol 6f :224 :46 1:113 ft *6-5e 1175 33 32 **21** 1no SmithT3 Ⓕ Ⓢ c12000 81 GoodHpes,LionTmr,HppyDys 12

STRETCH CALL The horse was second at this stage of the race, a length behind the leader. The stretch call is made about ⅛ mile from the finish.

30Jun81-6Hol 6f :224 :46 1:113 ft *6-5e 1175 33 32 21 **1no** SmithT3 Ⓕ Ⓢ c12000 81 GoodHpes,LionTmr,HppyDys 12

FINISH The horse finished first, a nose in front of the second horse. If second, third or unplaced, the superior figure indicates his margin behind the winner.

30Jun81-6Hol 6f :224 :46 1:113 ft *6-5e 1175 33 32 21 1no **SmithT3** Ⓕ Ⓢ c12000 81 GoodHpes,LionTmr,HppyDys 12

JOCKEY AND POST POSITION T Smith rode the horse, who started from post position number 3

30Jun81-6Hol 6f :224 :46 1:113 ft *6-5e 1175 33 32 21 1no SmithT3 Ⓕ Ⓢ **c12000** 81 GoodHpes,LionTmr,HppyDys 12

CLAIMING PRICE OR TYPE OF RACE The horse was entered to be claimed for $12,000 and the "c" indicates she was claimed; the Ⓢ indicates that the race was exclusively for fillies and mares, the Ⓢ a restricted race that is not for open company. If it is an allowance race other than maiden or starter, the purse is given. If it is a stakes race, the name of the race is given.

30Jun81-6Hol 6f :224 :46 1:113 ft *6-5e 1175 33 32 21 1no SmithT3 Ⓕ Ⓢ c12000 **81** GoodHpes,LionTmr,HppyDys 12

SPEED RATING The horse's speed rating was 81.

30Jun81-6Hol 6f :224 :46 1:113 ft *6-5e 1175 33 32 21 1no SmithT3 Ⓕ Ⓢ c12000 81 **GoodHpes,LionTmr,HppyDys** 12

FIRST THREE FINISHERS These are the first three finishers in the race

30Jun81-6Hol 6f :224 :46 1:113 ft *6-5e 1175 33 32 21 1no SmithT3 Ⓕ Ⓢ c12000 81 GoodHpes,LionTmr,HppyDys **12**

NUMBER OF STARTERS Twelve horses started in the race.

the Midwest is not usually ready to go up against those racing at Hollywood Park or Aqueduct. The better horses race where there is more money to be won.

Distance—Most horses prefer either short or long races. By checking the past performances (PPs), you can tell which type of distance has suited the horse in the past. (By the way, the standard distance measure used is the furlong, or eighth of a mile. So, 6F is three-quarters of a mile.)

Fractional Times—How fast did the horse run at the various stages of his last race? Is he fast enough to keep pace with his rivals in today's contest? Handicappers who live and die by this comparison are called *pace handicappers*.

Final Time—Perhaps needless to say, better horses run faster. The final time is the measure of this, but it is affected by those fractional times. If the race is run faster today in the early going than the horse is used to, he may tend to give up and not even equal the final time of his previous race.

Track Condition—Ever heard of mudders? As the Abbot and Costello routine pointed out, some horses look like world beaters when the track is "off." Dry tracks are listed as "fast." "Off" tracks include all other conditions from just after a rain, sloppy, and all of the in-between states. What's important is the history of your horse under the different track conditions. It's in his PPs.

Remember, all of this information is part of the expectation that history repeats itself. Horses that have reacted favorably to mud, or a shorter distance, or a longer rest between races in the past, are good bets to do so in the future.

Closing odds—Was the horse bet on last time out? Did he win at high odds? Did he fail as the favorite? When a horse runs better than the crowd expected you can be sure that the trainer was responsible. We'll talk about trainers later, but the pattern should be noted here.

Weight—Weight is used to equalize the contenders. It is assigned according to the record of money won or races won. Say the conditions of the race assign the horse 115 pounds. If the jockey weighs 114 and the saddle weighs two pounds, too bad—the horse will be announced as one pound overweight. If the jockey and saddle weigh 112 together, then lead is added to the saddle to make it 115 pounds. That's why they weigh the jockeys before *and* after the race. They don't want those lead bars littering the track while the race is being run.

The Calls—You can track the horse's progress through the running of the race by looking at the calls. The last call is always the finish, and the next-to-last call is always the beginning or the head of the stretch. Your interest here is whether or not the horse made any big effort and at what stage of the race he was trying. If he ran ten lengths behind the entire way, you'll need some outstanding reasoning to bet on him today. If he was close to the lead in the early part of the race, he is showing signs of life and may be ready for a better effort today. The key is *condition;* one of the most important factors in handicapping. A horse in top condition, like a conditioned athlete, is always a threat to win.

Jockey and Post Position—At most tracks all but a few of the jockeys will be able to get the job done if they have the best horse. Don't worry about it, but be aware that the best jockeys tend to get their choice of the better horses in each field. Post position, unlike in harness racing, makes little difference in most races.

Claiming Price—This line should be called class, and to most handicappers it is factor number one. But determining class lends itself to elements of opinion, just as in classes of people. Surely class has something to do with money won. Each race has a purse value to the winner, and the higher the purse the better the competition.

The three basic types of races are: claiming races, allowance races, and stakes and handicaps. In claiming races all horses entered are up for sale. They can be purchased (or claimed) for the stated price. So, you would not expect a horse who has run in claiming races of $12,500 to be competitive against $25,000 claimers. In allowance races the horses cannot be bought and the purses are higher than in most claiming races. Stakes and handicaps are the top rung of the ladder with the winner of races like the Arlington Million entitled to $600,000.

To recap class, as a horse goes up in class he faces better competition, and as he goes down his rivals are usually weaker. A move in either direction can greatly affect his chances of winning today.

Speed Ratings—These are a quickie index of the final time the horse ran as compared to the track record for that distance. In racing shorthand, one length equals one-fifth of a second. Therefore, if the winner ran six furlongs (3/4 mile) in one minute and 10 seconds (1:10) and your horse was second by three lengths (2^3), then your horse's final time adjusts to one minute and 10 and three-fifths seconds ($1:10^3$).

Back to the speed rating: If the track record for 6F is 1:09 or one minute and nine seconds, then the winner of the race we described was one second slower, because he ran a 1:10. One second equals five lengths, or five off the speed rating: His speed rating is 95. He beat our horse by three lengths, so our speed rating must be 92—not so bad. Speed ratings are quick comparisons of how fast horses have run lately, but be careful not to compare ratings for different distances to each other, or ratings from different tracks to each other, or ratings from fast tracks to ratings earned on "off" tracks. Ratings are just a tool, not the end-all.

The First Three Finishers—It's nice to know whether another horse in the field today has been able to consistently beat some, or all, of the other horses in today's race.

Number of Starters—A finish of fourth in a field of 12 means the horse outran eight horses. Fourth in a field of six means he beat only two.

One of the maxims of complete handicapping is that no information should be overlooked. All the bits and pieces should be digested in order to get the total picture—which brings us to the other use of the *Racing Form:* system play. This is much faster and easier; when making selections you need only scan the PPs for the horse whose records fits the system's few rules. All horses which qualify under these rules are bet without comparison to, or regard for, the other horses in the race. As an example, let's say the rules of your system are as follows:

(1) Play is restricted to claiming races only;

(2) The horse must have won his last race;

(3) He must have raced nine days ago or less;

(4) He must be carrying less weight today than in his last race.

Without going into the merits of this system or the manner in which these criteria were chosen (by the way, this is a powerful system in the winter months), the way to find the eligible horses is to scan only the top line, or most recent race, of each horse and look at the *finish position* only. If the horse was not first that's it—he's ineligible. Go on to the next set of PPs.

If he did win then slide your finger to the left side of the chart and check the *date* of his last race. Was it nine days ago or less? No? Elimination! Yes? Okay—slide right to the *weights* he carried in the race. More than today's assigned weight? Great—he's a play.

System horses must meet *all* criteria or no play is allowed. Because this system covers claiming races only (which is about two-thirds of the races on the day's card), checking the entire *Form* for that day takes 10 to 15 minutes, even for a novice player. Complete handicapping can take 30 minutes or more per race.

Complete handicapping, however, is thorough. All factors are considered, weighed and compared, and then a selection is made. System play may only select one or two horses a day; wagering is mechanical regardless of odds or the fact that there are two qualified horses in the same race.

By the way, if you are looking for help in selecting horses, you'll be offered plenty as you walk into the racetrack (in the form of tip and selection sheets). If those tipsters are so good, why do they sell for one or two dollars? What's even more insulting are their claims of success, which are inflated or aided by the selection of up to three horses in each race. These sheets will not make you any money.

The *Racing Form* has a panel of experts whose picks appear on the pages preceding the PPs for the first race. The value of these columns is not so much in the predictions they make, but in the comments the selectors like "Sweeps" make about the horses. These comments can reveal aspects which most of us will miss when reading the PPs.

On the very same page will appear the "trouble" notes. This column mentions the horses in each race who were blocked or stumbled or ran into some other form of bad racing luck in their last start. Naturally, this can be valuable information when trying to understand a bad performance.

Some other things to look for (refer to Table 11-2):

(1) Trainer—Horses are dumb, and jockeys are merely hired riders. Racing orders, jockey selection, strategy—and all of the important stuff in racing—are in the hands of the trainer. A serious bettor should study the trainers at the local track and learn their individual habits. Everyone who goes to the track should refer to the program's listing of the top ten trainers and jockeys. It makes sense to lean towards the "hot hands" at your track.

(2) Record—Even though it's still early in the year, *Daring Bet* is 0-1 in 1983 and 0-for-18 in 1982. That's a losing streak of 19 straight. Look at the record of *To Erin*. This horse is 5-for-9 in 1982. History tends to repeat itself.

(3) Claims—Horses running in claiming races are up for sale. As you can see in the PPs of *To Erin*, the current owner paid $20,000 for the horse on May 22 and proceeded to win with the horse in its very next start, only seven days later. Horses recently purchased should be watched.

(4) Workouts—There are plenty of sore and otherwise unhealthy horses running in every race. A sore horse cannot stand constant racing augmented by morning exercise or workouts. Therefore, the importance of workouts is not the speed but the frequency. Horses who work and race regularly are at least capable of winning. Workout lines which read:

Jan 4   Aqu   5f   ft   1:01³   h, would translate as

Table 11-2

To Erin
B. h. 7, by Epic Journey—Celty, by Swali II
Br.—Granger H C & Hazel D (Cole)
Own.—Lane G E
Tr.—Sedlacek Michael C
1125
$25,000
1982 9 5 0 3 $40,350
1981 10 4 4 1 $55,150
$6,750
Lifetime 61 18 10 16 $283,083   Turf 5 1 0 0

29May82-6Mth 1¼:48¹ 1:13² 1:47 sy *2-3 106⁵ 55½ 46½ 43½ 1ⁿᵒ LizarzaburuPM⁵ 70 To Erin, In Deep Water, Hagline 6
22May82-3Mth 1¼:49 1:13¹ 1:45 gd *4-5 116 1½ 1² 1⁷ 1⁵ Franklin R J⁴ c25000 80 To Erin, Brodi River, Recidian 8
8May82-3Mth 1 :46³ 1:11⁴ 1:38¹ft *4-5 119 6¹¹ 5⁶ 4⁵ 37½ Franklin R J⁴ 25000 74 Dragon Slayer, Adventure, To Erin 6
30Apr82-7Mth 1¹⁰:46² 1:11² 1:42¹ft 4½ 117 55½ 45 3³ 33½ Franklin R J¹ Aw15000 81 Pepp'sSgundo,TimlyCounsl,ToErin 8
10Apr82-8Kee 1¼:49⁴ 1:14² 1:45²ft *1 117 4² 2¹½ 1¹½ 15 Franklin R J⁵ 30000 79 ToErin,Belle'sRuler,WestrnBufflo 10
10Mar82-9FG 1¼:48¹ 1:12¹ 1:44¹ft 4½ 115 53½ 65½ 54½ 67½ Smith G P⁵ Aw15000 83 BoysNtOut,SwngagLght,Bobrobbry 8
7Feb82-9FG 1¼:47 1:11³ 1:44²gd 4 118 77⅞ 6⁵ 4⁵ 35 VsquezJ⁷ Louisiana H 85 Aspro, Withholding, To Erin 7
21Jan82-9FG 1¼:47² 1:13¹ 1:46 ft *2-5 116 37½ 2¹½ 1¹ 1² Franklin R J⁴ Aw13000 82 To Erin, Going Magic, Curribot 6
Jan 4 Aqu [·] 5f ft 1:01³ h   ●Dec 29 Med 5f ft 1:01 hg

Leader Of The Pack
B. g. 6, by Gold And Myrrh—Maggie Marble, by Sword Dancer
Br.—Haley C J Jr (Va)
Own.—Old Glory Stable
117
Tr.—DeBonis Robert
$25,000
1983 1 0 1 0 $2,500
1982 17 2 2 5 $26,995
Turf 5 0 0 0 $660
Lifetime 66 10 8 15 $113,181

1Jan83 3Med 1¼:47² 1:12 1:45²ft 2½e 113 11½ 1hd 2½ 2½ Miceli M¹ 22500 81 KnReson,Ldr0fThPck,EstrnCounsl 7
14Dec82-8Med 6f :22¹ :45 1:11¹ft 9½e 116 58½ 66⅞ 7⁹ 73½ Miceli M⁷ 25000 84 Tolerable,Adjudicdo,DifficileWriter 8
4Dec82-7Med 1¼:47⁴ 1:12 1:45²ft *8-5e 116 1½ 2¹ 3⁴ 55½ Miceli M⁶ 25000 76 GrtFnfr,DstngshdGnt,ChoosyBggr 11
16Nov82-9Med 1¼:46⁴ 1:11 1:45 ft *4-5e 116 2hd 2hd 2⁴ 35½ Miceli M⁶ 25000 78 BritishGunner,GrtFnfr,Ldr0fThPck 8
30Sep82-4Med 1¼ ①:46¹1:11 1:43 fm 4½ 115 2½ 2½ 10⁹ 11¹¹ LizrzburuPM¹¹ c25000 76 JustASnAway,UnconscousLd,Mnjhr 11
27Sep82-4Med 1¼:47³ 1:13¹ 1:46²sy 4½ 116 1¹ 12½ 2¹ 2ⁿᵒ Miceli M⁷ c20000 77 Cisk, LeaderOfThePack,LeaveWord 9
6Sep82-1Med 1¼:47 1:11³ 1:44 ft 4½ 116 1hd 11½ 2½ 33½ Miceli M⁶ 20000 85 DblWhmmy,RdHtndClLd0fThPck 8
21Aug82-3Mth 1 :47² 1:11³ 1:37 ft 9⅞ 114 75½ 8¹¹ 8¹⁶ 8²⁰ Miceli M⁶ 30000 68 Irish Tab, Sir Scan, Shaz 9
Jan 9 Bel tr.t 3f ft :38² b   Dec 1 Med 5f ft 1:01² h

Daring Bet
Dk. b. or br. g. 6, by Crimson Satan—Sure Thing 11, by High Hat
Br.—Clarke Mrs T & Sm (Ky)
Own.—MacMillen W C Jr
113
Tr.—Watters Sidney Jr
$20,000
1983 1 0 0 0
1982 18 0 2 3 $10,760
Turf 8 0 1 1 $5,800
Lifetime 66 10 8 15 $113,540 $660

3Jan83-2Aqu 1⁷⁰[·]:48¹1:13¹1:43⁴ft 8½ 117 9¹⁸ 8¹⁸ 7²¹ 6²² Molina V H¹ 25000 61 NoClear,RedHotndClr,Mr Nicefield 9
24Dec82-5Aqu 1⁷⁰[·]:49 1:14 1:44 ft 7 117 7¹⁰ 7¹⁰ 7⁹½ 6¹² Molina V H⁶ 25000 70 EvsiveJohn,OurCelticHir,Mr Nicfield 8
11Dec82-9Aqu 1½[·]:48²1:13³1:53¹ft 20 117 8¹¹ 88 3² 2⁴ Molina V H¹¹ 25000 76 Lrking'sRun,DrngBet,MsterForce 12
4Dec82-1Aqu 1¼[·]:47⁴1:12²1:44³gd 5 117 4⁸ 23½ 2⁵ 36½ Molina V H⁴ 20000 74 OurCelticHeir,RomanChel,DrngBet 7
24Nov82-9Aqu 1 :48 1:14 1:40¹ft 33 117 5³ 3½ 32½ 3² Molina V H⁸ 20000 63 Mr Nicefield,RomanChef,DrngBet 10
11Nov82-1Aqu 1 :46³ 1:11³ 1:37²ft 29 117 6³⅞ 86⅞ 8¹² 8¹¹ Molina V H² 25000 68 ChoosyBggr,RisABuck,SprtnMonk 8
30Oct82-1FH a2¼[S] 3:56¹fm 161 105⅞ 8⁷ 44⅞ 3⁶ SmithwickDMJr³ Mdn CrystlsChling,AqOfLitqton,DrngBt 12
Dec 29 Bel tr.t 4f ft :50 b   Dec 1 Bel tr.t 4f ft :47³ h   Nov 23 Bel 3f ft :36¹ h

Copyright © 1982, by *Daily Racing Form, Inc.* Reprinted with permission of copyright owner.

follows:

Date: January 4

Track: Aqueduct, NY

Distance: Five furlongs (5/8 of a mile)

Track Condition: Fast

Time: One minute and 1 and 3/5 seconds

Pace: Handily (under a firm but not all-out ride)

Becoming familiar with and recognizing the value of the material contained within the *Daily Racing Form* will give you the confidence you need to do your own handicapping. As with anything else, practice makes perfect!

Chapter 12

The Professional Harness Handicapper

by Hal Straus

From time to time I receive letters that go something like this: "I have been successfully betting the harness races at my local track. I am considering quitting my job and betting the horses full time. What do you think?"

The supposed life of a professional harness bettor sounds glamorous to the outsider. Joe the Pro spends his days at the track, king in his private box. As his adoring admirers beg him for even the smallest hint at a winner, Joe basks in their adulation, occasionally dispensing a crumb their way. Every so often Joe leaves his throne to wager, usually on a cold $150 exacta. The crowd stands in awe of Joe's brillance—and also of his ever-thickening wallet.

Let's look at reality.

Betting harness horses, bucking a 16 to 25% takeout, is a difficult way to make a living. Nobody cares if you lose—and lose you will, most of the time. (The trick is to win more on your good days than you lose on your bad ones.) You will at times lose eight consecutive photos. Your cinch of the season will be disqualified. Your admiring legions are usually tapped out desperadoes who mistake you for a loan company. You will experience excruciating boredom as you sit through a downpour watching $4000 claimers. You will spend months watching horses pace and trot around in circles, and quite possibly have nothing to show for it.

Away from the raceway, things may not be any better. Your wife wil threaten that if you spend one more day at the damn track, she's leaving. Your neighbors will sadly whisper about your addiction. The job you left, tedious though it may have been, starts to look better and better.

Still interested? Then ask yourself these questions: Do I really enjoy racing? Am I a good enough handicapper to beat the high takeout and daily expenses? Do I enjoy poring over charts and figures? Am I organized? Can I survive the bad times, as well as the neighbors? Can I control myself at the track? Is my bankroll sufficient both to bet big (nobody makes a living betting $10 a race) and to withstand a losing streak? Do I have the time to devote myself fully to the task?

This last point is often overlooked. There are no shortcuts to success in the racing game. It demands total dedication. Those who expect to work shorter hours as a professional handicapper will be quickly disappointed.

The hours spent at the raceway are only part of the working week. Because there is so much to do at the track—observe warmups, check the tote board, watch and make notes on the races, bet, study the replays—you must do your handicapping before you get to the track. You need also attend qualifiers, read harness magazines, study charts, and keep notebooks (everything from mud statistics to trainer records). This doesn't include hanging out at the local horsemen's bar or visiting the racing office or attending horse auctions.

Playing the harness races professionally is a full-time job. Let's follow Joe the Pro through a day of his business—betting the harness races.

It is qualifier day. After a quick breakfast, Joe leaves his house at 10 a.m. for the 20-minute drive to Surething Raceway. By the time he parks, obtains an entry sheet, and gets to his seat, it is almost 10:30, post time for the first qualifying race.

Through his binoculars, Joe watches all seven non-betting events, jotting notes. Though more than 40 horses compete in the qualifiers this day, only one—a newly arrived Down Under pacer which finished third in the fifth race under a strong hold—attracts Joe's interest.

It is now 11:40. Because a friend has listed Joe as part owner of one of his horses, Joe receives free parking and admission, and a stable pass. He now uses the latter to visit the racing office, where he examines the bulletin board. An index card announces a filly for sale for $5000; noting that the animal is a first-time starter in a later race, Joe concludes that she isn't much. Joe also sees a trainer friend of his and they exchange information (because he is in the grandstand every night watching every horse, Joe invariably knows more about most horses than the trainer does).

Leaving the grounds, Joe stops to buy a program. It contains not only tonight's past performances, but also the chart of last night's races. When Joe gets home at 12:45, he takes out his file and compares the program chart with his own notes, looking for discrepancies. Later this evening, he will view a tape of last night's races one more time to answer any lingering questions.

Fortunately, Surething Raceway maintains up-to-date driver and post statistics. However, it provides no information on trainers. Because of this, Joe keeps a detailed book on trainers. Every day, he enters data on every trainer who had a horse entered the previous night. For each, Joe not only records where his horse finished but also notes facts about class, betting action, layoffs, and driver changes.

By now it is 1:30, time for a quick lunch. While he eats, Joe glances through the latest copy of *Horseman and Fair World*, a weekly magazine that prints national harness results. Joe also reads the trot column in the local newspaper.

Joe is now ready to attack tonight's program. He keeps a stack of recent programs and charts by his side. In the opening race, a first-time starter is entered, so Joe checks his notebook to see how the trainer has fared with his previous newcomers. In the fifth, Joe spots a new driver he's never heard of; he looks up the man's record in the latest edition of the USTA Roster of

Harness Racing Drivers.

In the seventh, a shipper from an out-of-town track looks like a contender, so Joe thumbs through back issues of his magazine to determine the quality of the visitor's recent opposition. In the eighth, Joe looks through his old program notes to see whether the rail horse's apparently dull last effort was due to trouble. In the ninth, when Joe discovers a horse who recorded a particularly swift time last week, Joe pulls out his charts to see whether that night's other clockings were uncommonly swift.

By 3:30, Joe has finished his handicapping. He has constructed an odds line for each race, as well as written down some possible exacta or trifecta plays. He doesn't yet know for certain which horses he may bet, since much will depend on the final odds.

Joe has some ideas, though. A colt in the fourth race, which Joe hates, is usually well-backed by the public. Joe thinks there may be a chance for an exacta score. In the seventh, one pacer ran into all kinds of difficulty last week although the chart line doesn't show it; Joe feels the horse might be let away at 6-1 rather than the 2-1 he thinks the horse is really worth. In the last exacta, Joe thinks the solid-looking 5 horse will leave and slow the pace, leading to a 5-1 or 5-2 exacta.

Joe now has but 90 minutes before dinnertime to run the rest of his life. He dines early, so he can arrive at the track by 6 p.m. The races don't start until 7:30, but Joe wants to eyeball the early workouts and once again go over last night's replays.

Packing his folder—which includes two pens, paper, a stopwatch, binoculars, tonight's program, his file of programs and charts, and a special pad on which Joe records daily-double and exacta possibles—Joe returns to the racetrack once again.

At the track, he chooses a seat high above the finish line to better observe the entire field at all times. Joe checks the information board on which are posted scratches and late driver changes. In the first race, the logical front-runner has been scratched, so Joe revises his entire line. In the eighth, a weak driver has been replaced by one of the meeting's best drivers, and again Joe must do a complete re-evaluation of the race.

Joe does this as he watches the early warmups. He sees a long shot in the third which looks especially powerful. But after looking over the program again, Joe dismisses the horse one more time.

The replays from last night begin. Joe takes out both last night's program and the chart printed on the back of tonight's program. He observes the replays, with one eye on the workouts that are taking place simultaneously. Later, he grabs a soft drink (no liquor on the job) before returning to his seat.

By now it is ten minutes to post time for the first race. Joe records the daily-double possibilities but sees no particularly attractive combinations. He also checks the board for possible overlays not only in the win pool, but also in the place and show departments.

During each race, Joe will take notes. After each contest, he will record the final odds of each horse, then watch the replay for anything he may have missed during the race. He will also be checking the upcoming warmups, as well as any tote activity.

This is his night:

1st race—No bet. Race is won by #5, a 4-1 shot whom Joe had rated 6-1. As Joe had figured, the first-time starter was nowhere.

2nd race—An 8-1 morning-line pacer is getting hammered down to 8-5, but Joe decides not to chase it. The horse wins. Joe observes that the second choice was stuck behind a dead horse until late.

3rd race—The cheap filly from the morning bulletin board is an underlaid 4-1, but Joe can't find any bargains in either the win or in the exacta pools. A 5-2 shot wins the race, while the longshot Joe had observed earlier finishes a creditable fourth.

4th race—As Joe had predicted, the public bangs down the weak favorite, #2, to 7-5. Joe finds some big exacta payoffs with the two horses he likes, #3 and #6. He invests $100 in the race, playing 3-6 and 6-3 heavily and also using 3-1. 3-5, 6-1, and 6-5. He has a shot to win more than $1000. The favorite runs poorly, but #1 noses out 3 and 6 in a blanket photo.

5th race—No bet. Joe does see a mare which has to steady throughout the stretch, and marks her as a pacer to watch.

6th race—A horse Joe had rated at 3-1 is let away at 7-1, so Joe bets $110 to win on him. The horse races well, leaving and then going without cover to finish a game third.

7th race—The horse that Joe had marked in the afternoon goes off at 9-5. No bet. The horse finishes fifth. Another horse, returning from a layoff, is raced gingerly but appears to be coming back to form.

8th race—A horse Joe had liked a little had warmed up poorly, and nobody else looked good. No bet. The race is won by a horse that showed absolutely nothing previously until tonight's wakeup at 15-1. Joe shrugs. He notes one pacer that was four-wide around the final turn.

9th race—Joe is disappointed to find that a $3 exacta ticket on the 5-1 combination is returning only $12, and the 5-2 only $14. If he plays them both, he'd be getting barely even money for his exacta bet—assuming it won. His key horse is 4 to 5, no bargain. No bet. The winning combination is indeed 5-1.

By the time Joe returns home, it is nearly midnight, the end of a racing day that began 14 hours earlier. He takes a few minutes to record his bets and expenses for the evening. Even though Joe lost $200 this night, he may have spotted an upcoming goodie overlooked by the bulk of the public.

By limiting his bets only to worthwhile overlays, Joe has maximized his chance for long-term profits. What counts for the professional bettor, as Joe the Pro knows, is not any particular night, but how the bank book looks at the end of the year.

Full-time harness bettors are rare creatures. Unless you can win enough at harness betting to surpass your earnings from your regular job, chuck the notion that such a life is for you. The fact is far less attractive than the myth.

KEEPING YOUR GAMING
KNOWLEDGE CURRENT

Now that you know how to beat the propositions in the casino, the sports book, and at the track, it's important to keep abreast of the rapid and continuous changes and developments in these areas. The best way to do that is with a subscription to *Gambling Times* magazine.

Since February of 1977, readers of *Gambling Times* magazine have profited immensely. They have done so by using the information they have read each month. If that sounds like a simple solution to winning more and losing less, well it is! Readers look to *Gambling Times* for that very specific reason. And it delivers.

Gambling Times is totally dedicated to showing readers how to win more money in every form of legalized gambling. How much you're going to win depends on many factors, but it's going to be considerably more than the cost of a subscription.

WINNING AND MONEY

Winning, that's what *Gambling Times* is all about. And money, that's what *Gambling Times* is all about. Because winning and money go hand in hand.

Here's what the late Vince Lombardi, the famous football coach of the Green Bay Packers, had to say about winning:

"It's not a sometime thing. Winning is a habit. There is no room for second place. There is only one place in my game and that is first place. I have finished second twice in my time at Green Bay and I don't ever want to finish second again. The objective is to win—fairly, squarely, decently, by the rules—but to win. To beat the other guy. Maybe that sounds hard or cruel. I don't think it is. It is and has always been an American zeal to be first in anything we do, and to win, and to win and to win."

Mr. Lombardi firmly believed that being a winner is "man's finest hour." *Gambling Times* believes it is too, while being a loser is depressing, ego-deflating, expensive and usually very lonely. "Everybody loves a winner" may be a cliche, but it's true. Winners command respect and are greatly admired. Winners are also very popular and have an abundance of friends. You may have seen a winner in a casino, with a bevy of girls surrounding him...or remember one who could get just about any girl he wanted.

Some of the greatest gamblers in the world also have strong views on what winning is all about. Here's what two of them have to say on the subject:

"To be a winner, a man has to feel good about himself and know he has some kind of advantage going in. I never made bets on even chances. Smart is better than lucky."— "Titanic" Thompson

"When it comes to winnin', I got me a one-track mind. You gotta want to win more than anything else. And you gotta have confidence. You can't pretend to have it. That's no good. You gotta have it. You gotta know. Guessers are losers. Gamblin's just as simple as that."—Johnny Moss

Gambling Times will bring you the knowledge you need to come home a winner and come home in the money. For it is knowledge, the kind of knowledge you'll get in its pages, that separates winners from losers. It's winning and money that *Gambling Times* offers you. *Gambling Times* will be your working manual to winning wealth.

The current distribution of this magazine is limited to selected newsstands in selected cities. Additionally, at newsstands where it is available, it's being snapped up, as soon as it's displayed, by gamblers who know a sure bet when they see one.

So if you're serious about winning, you're best off subscribing to *Gambling Times*. Then you can always count on its being there, conveniently delivered to your mailbox—and what's more, it will be there one to two weeks before it appears on the newsstands. You'll be among the first to receive the current issue as soon as it comes off the presses, and being first is the way to be a winner.

Having every monthly issue of *Gambling Times* will enable you to build an "Encyclopedia of Gambling," since the contents of this magazine are full of sound advice that will be as good in five or ten years as it is now.

As you can see, a subscription to *Gambling Times* is your best bet for a future of knowledgeable gambling. It's your ticket to *WINNING* and *MONEY.*

Take the time to read the following offer. As you can see, *Gambling Times* has gone all out to give you outstanding bonuses. You can join the knowledgeable players who have learned that *Gambling Times* helps them to win more money.

FOUR NEW WAYS TO GET 12 WINNING ISSUES OF *GAMBLING TIMES* FREE...

Every month over 250,000 readers trust *Gambling Times* to introduce powerful new winning strategies and systems. Using proven scientific methods, the world's leading experts show you how to win big money in the complex field of gambling.

Gambling Times has shown how progressive slot machines can be beat. Readers have discovered important new edges in blackjack. They've been shown how to know for sure when an opponent is bluffing at poker. *Gambling Times* has also spelled out winning methods for football, baseball and basketball. They've published profound new ways of beating horses. Their team of experts will uncover information in the months ahead that's certain to be worth thousands of dollars to you.

In fact, the features are so revolutionary that they must take special precautions to make sure *Gambling Times* readers learn these secrets long before anyone else. So how much is *Gambling Times* worth to you? Well...

NOW *GAMBLING TIMES* CAN BE BETTER THAN FREE! Here's how: This BONUS package comes AUTOMATICALLY TO YOU WHEN YOU SUBSCRIBE...or goes to a friend if you give a gift subscription.

(1)   POKER BONUS at the TROPICANA card room in Las Vegas.
        Play poker at the TROPICANA and receive a free dinner buffet

and comps to the "Folies Bergere" show for you *and* a guest. Value exceeds $40 excluding gratuities.

(2) FREE SPORTS BET. CHURCHILL DOWNS SPORTS BOOK in Las Vegas will let you make one wager up to $300 with no "vigorish." This means instead of laying the usual 11-to-10 odds, you can actually bet even up! You can easily save $30 here.

(3) PAYOFF BIGGER THAN THE TRACK. LEROY'S RACE BOOK, in Las Vegas, will add 10% to your payoff (up to $30 extra) on a special bet. Just pick the horse and the race of your choice, anywhere in America. For the first time in history, you can win more than the track pays.

(4) OUTSTANDING ROOM DISCOUNTS available only to *Gambling Times* subscribers. Check in at the SANDS in Las Vegas or Atlantic City, the TROPICANA in Atlantic City, the HIGH SIERRA in Lake Tahoe, or the CONDADO INN & CASINO in San Juan, Puerto Rico. Stay for 3 days and 2 nights and you'll save $29 off their normal low rates.

THAT'S A SAVING GREATER THAN THE ENTIRE COST OF YOUR SUBSCRIPTION.

USE ALL FOUR CERTIFICATES (VALID FOR ONE YEAR)...GET *GAMBLING TIMES* FREE...AND YOU'LL PUT $93 IN YOUR POCKET!

To begin your delivery of *Gambling Times* magazine at once, enclose a payment of $36.00 by check or money order (U.S. currency), Master-Card or Visa. Add $5.00 per year for postage outside the United States.

Send payment to:

GAMBLING TIMES MAGAZINE
1018 N. Cole Avenue
Hollywood, California 90038

GAMBLING TIMES
MONEY BACK GUARANTEE

If at any time you decide *Gambling Times* is not for you, you will receive a full refund on all unmailed copies. You are under no obligation and may keep the bonus as a gift.

Other Valuable Sources of Knowledge
Available Through *Gambling Times*

(See ordering information on page 135.)

Here are some additional sources you can turn to for worthwhile gambling information:

The Experts Sports Handicapping Newsletter.

Published monthly, this newsletter will show you how to become an Expert handicapper. You will learn the different styles of handicapping and be able to select the one method best suited to your personality. Yearly subscriptions are $60; $50 for *Gambling Times* subscribers.

The Experts Blackjack Newsletter.

This monthly newsletter has all the top blackjack Experts working just for you. Features answers, strategies and insights that were never before possible. Yearly subscriptions are $60; $50 for *Gambling Times* subscribers.

Poker Player.

Published every other week, this *Gambling Times* newspaper features the best writers and theorists on the poker scene today. You will learn all aspects of poker, from odds to psychology, as well as how to play in no-limit competition and in tournaments. Yearly subscriptions (26 issues) are $20.

Casino Marketing International.

CMI sponsors the largest prize-pool blackjack tournaments in the world. Using an exciting non-elimination format, CMI offers the tournament blackjack player the opportunity to play in each round of the tournament. In 1984 the Desert Inn in Las Vegas hosted the Blackjack Tournaments. In 1985 CMI expects to offer Blackjack Tournaments in Atlantic City and Reno/Lake Tahoe. For information on where and when the next tournaments will be held, write CMI, 8462 Sunset Boulevard, Penthouse Suite, Los Angeles, CA 90069, or call toll free (800) 421-4442. In California call (800) 252-7772.

OTHER BOOKS AVAILABLE

If you can't find the following books at your local bookstore, they may be ordered directly from *Gambling Times,* 1018 N. Cole Ave., Hollywood, CA 90038. Information on how to order is on page 135.

Poker Books

According to Doyle by Doyle Brunson—Acknowledged by most people as the world's best all-around poker player, twice World Champion Doyle Brunson brings you his homespun wisdom from over 30 years as a professional poker player. This book will not only show you how to win at poker, it will give you valuable insights into how to better handle that poker game called LIFE.
Softbound. $6.95. (ISBN: 0-89746-003-0)

Caro on Gambling by Mike Caro—The world's leading poker writer covers all the aspects of gambling from his regular columns in *Gambling Times* magazine and *Poker Player* newspaper. Discussing odds and probabilities, bluffing and raising, psychology and character, this book will bring to light valuable concepts that can be turned into instant profits in home games as well as in the poker palaces of the West.
Softbound. $6.95. (ISBN: 0-89746-029-4)

Caro's Book of Tells by Mike Caro—The photographic body language of poker. Approximately 150 photographs with text explaining when a player is bluffing, when he's got the winning hand—and WHY. Based on accurate investigation; it is NOT guesswork. Even the greatest of gamblers has some giveaway behavior. For the first time in print, one of the world's top poker players reveals how he virtually can read minds because nearly every player has a "tell." Seal the leaks in your poker game and empty your opponent's chip tray.
Hardbound. $20.00. (ISBN: 0-914314-04-1)

The Gambling Times Official Rules of Poker by Mike Caro—Settles home poker arguments. Caro has written the revised rule book (including a section on etiquette) for the Horseshoe Club in Gardena, California, that may soon be adopted by other clubs and become the California standard. He is presently scheduling a meeting of poker room managers

at the Bingo Palace in Las Vegas. This should lead to the creation of a uniform book of rules for Nevada cardrooms. *The Gambling Times Official Rules of Poker* includes sections of the rules from public cardrooms, but mostly it is for home poker. The book is needed because there presently exists no true authority for settling Friday night poker disputes.
Softbound. $5.95. (ISBN: 0-89746-012-X)

Poker for Women by Mike Caro—How women can take advantage of the special male-female ego wars at the poker table and win. This book also has non-poker everyday value for women. Men can be destroyed at the poker table by coy, cunning or aggressive women. That's because, on a subconscious level, men expect women to act traditionally. This book tells women when to flirt, when to be tough and when to whimper. Many of the tactics are tried and proven by Caro's own students. This book does not claim that women are better players, merely that there are strategies available to them that are not available to their male opponents.
Softbound. $5.95. (ISBN: 0-89746-009-X)

Poker Without Cards by Mike Caro—Applying world-class poker tactics to everyday life. Is the salesman bluffing? Can you get a better price? Negotiating is like playing a poker hand. Although poker tactics are common in daily encounters, few people realize when a hand is being played. It's hard to make the right decision when you're not even aware that you've been raised. The book is honest and accurate in its evaluation of behavior.
Softbound. $6.95. (ISBN: 0-89746-038-3)

Wins, Places, and Pros by Tex Sheahan—With more than 50 years of experience as a professional poker player and cardroom manager/tournament director, Tex lets his readers in on the secrets that separate the men from the boys at the poker table. Descriptions of poker events, playing experiences from all over the world, and those special personalities who are the masters of the game. . .Tex knows them all and lays it out in his marvelous easy-to-read style.
Softbound. $6.95. (ISBN: 0-89746-008-1)

Blackjack Books

The Beginner's Guide to Winning Blackjack by Stanley Roberts—The world's leading blackjack writer shows beginners to the game how to obtain an instant advantage through the simplest of techniques. Covering Basic Strategy for all major casino areas from Las Vegas to the Bahamas, Atlantic City and Reno/Tahoe, Roberts provides a simple system to immediately know when the remaining cards favor the player. The entire method can be learned in less than two hours and taken to the casinos to produce sure profits.
Softbound. $10.00. (ISBN: 0-89746-014-6)

The Gambling Times Guide to Blackjack by Stanley Roberts with Edward O. Thorp, Ken Uston, Lance Humble, Arnold Snyder, Julian Braun, Richard Canfield and other experts in this field—The top blackjack authorities have been brought together for the first time to bring to the reader the ins and outs of the game of blackjack. All aspects of the game are discussed. Winning techniques are presented for beginners and casual players.
Softbound. $5.95. (ISBN: 0-89746-015-4)

Million Dollar Blackjack by Ken Uston—Every blackjack enthusiast or gaming traveler who fancies himself a "21" player can improve his game with this explosive bestseller. Ken Uston shows you how he and his team won over 4 million dollars at blackjack. Now, for the first time, you can find out how he did it and how his system can help you. Includes playing and betting strategies, winning secrets, protection from cheaters, Uston's Advanced Point Count System, and a glossary of inside terms used by professionals.
Hardbound. $18.95. (ISBN: 0-914314-08-4)

Casino Games

The Gambling Times Guide to Casino Games by Len Miller—The co-founder and editor of *Gambling Times* magazine vividly describes the casino games and explains their rules and betting procedures. This easy-to-follow guide covers blackjack, craps, roulette, keno, video machines, progressive slots and more. After reading this book, you'll play like a pro!
Softbound. $5.95. (ISBN: 0-89746-017-0)

The Gambling Times Guide to Craps by N.B. Winkless, Jr.—The ultimate craps book for beginners and experts alike. It provides you with a program to tackle the house edge that can be used on a home computer. This text shows you which bets to avoid and tells you the difference between craps in Nevada and craps in other gaming resort areas. It includes a glossary of terms and a directory of dealer schools.
Softbound. $5.95. (ISBN: 0-89746-013-8)

General Interest Books

According to Gambling Times: The Rules of Gambling Games by Stanley Roberts—At last you can finally settle all the arguments regarding what the rules are in every known gambling endeavor. From pari-mutuels to bookie slips, from blackjack to gin rummy, the rules of the games and the variations that are generally accepted in both public and private situations are clearly enumerated by the world's #1 gaming authority.
Hardbound. $12.00. (ISBN: 0-914314-07-6)

The Gambling Times Guide to Gaming Around the World compiled by Arnold L. Abrams—The complete travel guide to legal gaming throughout the world. This comprehensive gaming guide lists casinos around the world; the games played in each; cardrooms and facilities; greyhound racing and horse racing tracks, as well as jai alai frontons, lotteries and sports betting facilities. This book is a must for the traveling gamer.
Softbound. $5.95. (ISBN: 0-89746-020-0)

The Gambling Times Guide to Systems That Win, Volume I and Volume II—For those who want to broaden their gambling knowledge, this two-volume set offers complete gambling systems used by the experts. Learn their strategies and how to incorporate them into your gambling style. **Volume I** covers 12 systems that win for roulette, craps, backgammon, slot machines, horse racing, baseball, basketball and football.
Softbound. $5.95. (ISBN: 0-89746-034-0)
Volume II features 12 more systems that win, covering horse racing, craps, blackjack, slot machines, jai alai and baseball.
Softbound. $5.95. (ISBN: 0-89746-034-0)

The Gambling Times Guide to Winning Systems, Volume I and Volume II—For those who take their gambling seriously, *Gambling Times* presents a two-volume set of proven winning systems. Learn how the experts beat the house edge and become consistent winners. **Volume I** contains 12 complete strategies for casino games and sports wagering, including baccarat, blackjack, keno, basketball and harness handicapping.
Softbound. $5.95. (ISBN: 0-89746-032-4)
Volume II contains 12 more winning systems covering poker bluffing, pitching analysis, greyhound handicapping and roulette.
Softbound. $5.95. (ISBN: 0-89746-033-2)

Gambling Times Presents Winning Systems and Methods, Volume I—This collection of winning strategies by some of the nation's leading experts on gambling will help you in your quest to beat the percentages. **Volume I** includes several chapters on blackjack, as well as methods for beating baseball, basketball, hockey, steeplechase and grass racing.
Softbound. $5.95. (ISBN: 0-89746-036-7)

The Mathematics of Gambling by Edward O. Thorp—The "Albert Einstein of gambling" presents his second book on the subject. His first book, *Beat The Dealer,* set the gambling world on its heels and struck fear into the cold-blooded hearts of Las Vegas casino-owners in 1962. Now, more than twenty years later, Dr. Thorp again challenges the odds by bringing out a simple to understand version of more than thirty years of exploration into all aspects of what separates winners from losers. . .knowing the real meaning of the parameters of the games.
Softbound. $7.95. (ISBN: 0-89746-019-7)

Odds: Quick and Simple by Mike Caro—How to know the right lines and win by figuring the odds logically. Common sense replaces mathematical formulas. This book will teach probabilities plainly and powerfully. The emphasis will be on gambling, showing how to quickly determine whether or not to make a wager. Particular emphasis will be on sports bets, pot odds in poker, dice and various proposition bets. Also included will be tables of the most important gambling odds (craps, roulette, poker, blackjack, keno) for easy reference.
Softbound. $5.95. (ISBN: 0-89746-030-8)

P$yching Out Vegas by Marvin Karlins, Ph.D.—The dream merchants who build and operate gaming resorts subtly work on the casino patron to direct his attention, control his actions and turn his pockets inside out. At last, their techniques are revealed to you by a noted psychologist who shows you how you can successfully control your behavior and turn a losing attitude into a lifetime winning streak.
Hardbound. $12.00. (ISBN: 0-914314-03-3)

Winning by Computer by Dr. Donald Sullivan—Now, for the first time, the wonders of computer technology are harnessed for the gambler. Dr. Sullivan explains how to figure the odds and identify key factors in all forms of race and sports handicapping.
Softbound. $5.95. (ISBN: 0-89746-018-9)

Sports Betting Books

The Gambling Times Guide to Basketball Handicapping by Barbara Nathan—This easy-to-read, highly informative book is the definitive guide to basketball betting. Expert sports handicapper Barbara Nathan provides handicapping knowledge, insightful coverage, and step-by-step guidance for money management. The advantages and disadvantages of relying on sports services are also covered.
Softbound. $5.95. (ISBN: 0-89746-023-5)

The Gambling Times Guide to Football Handicapping by Bob McCune—Starting with the novice's approach to handicapping football, and winding up with some of the more sophisticated team selection techniques in the sports handicapping realm, this book will actually tell the reader how to forecast, *in advance,* the final scores of most major national football games. The author's background and expertise on the subject will put money into any sports gambler's pocket.
Softbound. $5.95. (ISBN: 0-89746-022-7)

The Gambling Times Guide to Greyhound Racing by William E. McBride—This complete discussion of greyhound racing is a must for anyone who is just beginning to appreciate this exciting and profitable sport. The book begins with a brief overview detailing the origins of greyhound racing and pari-mutuel betting, and explains the greyhound track environment, betting procedures, and handicapping methods. In-

cludes an appendix of various greyhound organizations, a review of greyhound books, and an interesting section on famous dogs and personalities in the world of greyhound racing.
Softbound. $5.95. (ISBN: 0-89746-007-3)

The Gambling Times Guide to Harness Racing by Igor Kusyshyn, Ph.D., Al Stanley and Sam Dragich—Three of Canada's top harness handicapping authorities present their inside approach to analyzing the harness racing scene and selecting winners. All the important factors from the type of sulky, workouts, drivers' ratings, speed, pace, etc., are skillfully presented in simple terms that can be used by novices and experienced racegoers to find the likely winners.
Softbound. $5.95. (ISBN: 0-89746-002-2)

The Gambling Times Guide to Jai Alai by William R. Keevers—The most comprehensive book on jai alai available. Author Bill Keevers takes the reader on an informative journey from the ancient beginnings of the game to its current popularity. This easy-to-understand guide will show you the fine points of the game, how to improve your betting percentage, and where to find jai alai frontons.
Softbound. $5.95. (ISBN: 0-89746-010-3)

The Gambling Times Guide to Thoroughbred Racing by R.G. Denis— Newcomers to the racetrack and veterans alike will appreciate the informative description of the thoroughbred pari-mutuel activity supplied by this experienced racing authority. Activities at the track and available information are blended skillfully in this guide to selecting winners that pay off in big-ticket returns.
Softbound. $5.95. (ISBN: 0-89746-005-7)

UPCOMING *GAMBLING TIMES* BOOKS

The following books will be at your local bookstore by September, 1984. If you can't find them there, they may also be ordered directly from *Gambling Times*.

Poker Books

Caro's Poker Encyclopedia by Mike Caro—Features alphabetical definitions and discussions of poker terms. Extensively cross-indexed, it can be used as a reference book to look up important poker terms (ante, bluff, sandbag) or it can be pleasurably read straight through. The definitions are brief; the advice is in-depth.
Softbound. $8.95. (ISBN: 0-89746-039-1)

Free Money: How to Win in the Cardrooms of California by Michael Wiesenberg—Computer expert and poker writer par excellence, Michael Wiesenberg delivers critical knowledge to those who play in the poker rooms of the western states. Wiesenberg gives you the precise meaning of the rules as well as the mathematics of poker to aid public and private poker players alike. Wiesenberg, a prolific author, is published by more gaming periodicals than any other writer.
Softbound. $6.95. (ISBN: 0-89746-027-8)

The Railbird by Rex Jones—The ultimate kibitzer, the man who watches from the rail in the poker room, has unique insights into the character and performance of all poker players. From this vantage point, Rex Jones, Ph.D., blends his expertise and considerable education in anthropology with his lifetime of poker playing and watching. The result is a delightful book with exceptional values for those who want to avoid the fatal errors of bad players and capitalize upon the qualities that make up the winning strengths of outstanding poker players.
Softbound. $6.95. (ISBN: 0-89746-028-6)

Tales Out of Tulsa by Bobby Baldwin—Oklahoma-born Bobby Baldwin, the youngest player to ever win the World Championship of Poker, is considered to be among the top five poker players in the world. Known affectionately as "The Owl," this brilliant poker genius, wise beyond his years, brings the benefits of his experience to the pages of this book.

It's sure to stop the leaks in your poker game, and you will be amazingly ahead of your opponents in the very next game you play.
Softbound. $6.95. (ISBN: 0-89746-006-5)

World Class Poker, Play by Play by Mike Caro—Once again, Caro brings the world of poker to life. This time he gives us a one-card-at-a-time analysis of world class poker, with many card illustrations. This book includes discussions of professional tactics, then simulates game situations and asks the reader to make decisions. Next, Caro provides the answer and the hand continues. This learn-while-you-pretend-to-play format is a favorite teaching method of Caro's and one which meets with a great deal of success.
Hardbound. $20.00. (ISBN: 0-914314-06-08)

General Interest Books

Caro on Computer Gambling by Mike Caro—Caro discusses computers and how they will change gambling. He provides winning systems and descriptions of actual programs. This book will give the novice a taste of how computers work. Using the Pascal programming language, Caro builds a working program step-by-step to show how a computer thinks and, also, how a human should analyze gambling propositions. This book is only slightly technical and mostly logical. Also discussed are ways that computers can cheat and speculation on the future of computers in gambling. Will you be able to type in your horse bets from your home computer? Can that personal computer be linked by phone into a perpetual poker game with the pots going straight into your bank account? The answers to these questions are found right here in Caro's book.
Softbound. $6.95. (ISBN: 0-89746-042-1)

The Gambling Times Quiz Book by Mike Caro—Learn while testing your knowledge. Caro's book includes questions and answers on the concepts and information published in previous issues of *Gambling Times*. Caro tells why an answer is correct and credit is given to the author whose *Gambling Times* article suggested the question. This book covers only established fact, not the personal opinions of authors, and Caro's inimitable style makes this an easy-reading, easy-learning book.
Softbound. $5.95. (ISBN: 0-89746-031-6)

How the Superstars Gamble by Ron Delpit—Follow the stars to the racetracks, ball games, casinos and private clubs. You'll be amazed at how involved these world famous personalities are in the gambling scene, and how clever they are at the games they play. Ron Delpit, lifelong horse racing fan and confidant of innumerable showbiz greats, tells you fascinating tales about his friends, the superstars, with startling heretofore secret facts.
Hardbound. $12.00. (ISBN: 0-914314-17-3)

How to Win at Gaming Tournaments by Haven Earle Haley—Win your share of the millions of dollars and fabulous prizes being awarded to gaming contestants, and have the glory of being a World Champion. Poker, gin rummy, backgammon, craps, blackjack and baccarat are all popular tournament games. The rules, special tournament regulations, playing procedures, and how to obtain free entry are fully explained in this informative manual. The tournament promoters—who they are, where they hold events—and the cash and prizes awarded are explained in detail. Tournament play usually requires special strategy changes, which are detailed in this book.
Softbound. $8.95. (ISBN: 0-89746-016-2)

You're Comped: How to Be a Casino Guest by Len Miller—If you're a player you don't have to pay! Learn how to be "comped" in luxury casino-resort hotels the world over. A list of casinos together with names and addresses of junket representatives are included in this revealing guidebook. How to handle yourself on a junket is important if you want to receive all that you've been promised and be invited back again. How to do this, along with what you can expect from the casino, is explained in detail.
Softbound. $7.95. (ISBN: 0-89746-041-3)

Sports Betting Books

Fast Track to Harness Racing Profits by Mark Cramer——This systematic analysis of nuances in past performances will uncover patterns of improvement which will lead to flat bet profits. This book provides a functioning balance between creative handicapping and mechanical application.
Softbound. $6.95. (ISBN: 0-89746-026-X)

Fast Track to Thoroughbred Profits by Mark Cramer—A unique approach to selecting winners, with price in mind, by distinguishing between valuable and common-place information. Results: higher average pay-offs and solid flat bet profits. How to spot signs of improvement and when to cash in. And much, much more.
Softbound. $6.95. (ISBN: 0-89746-025-1)

Ordering Information

Send your book order along with your check or money order to:

Gambling Times
1018 N. Cole Ave.
Hollywood, CA 90038

Softbound Books: Please add $1.00 per book if delivered in the United States, $1.50 in Canada or Mexico, and $3.50 for foreign countries.

Hardbound Books: Shipping charges for the following books are $2.50 if delivered in the United States, $3.00 in Canada or Mexico, and $5.00 for foreign countries:
According to Gambling Times: The Rules of Gambling Games
Caro's Book of Tells
How the Superstars Gamble
Million Dollar Blackjack
P$yching Out Vegas
World Class Poker, Play by Play